IMAGES OF AUSTRALIA

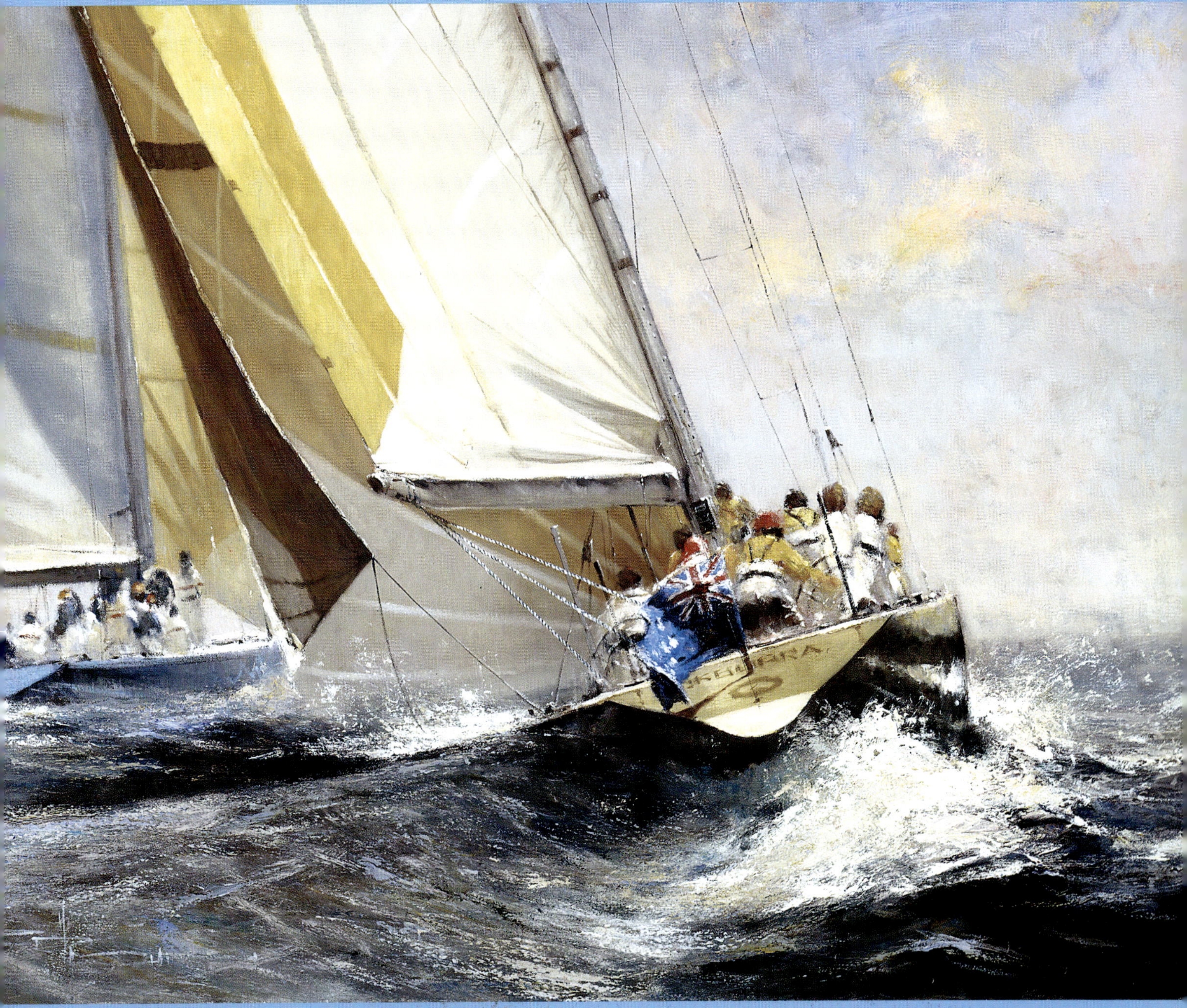

IAS

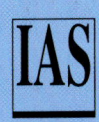

by
Robert Hagan

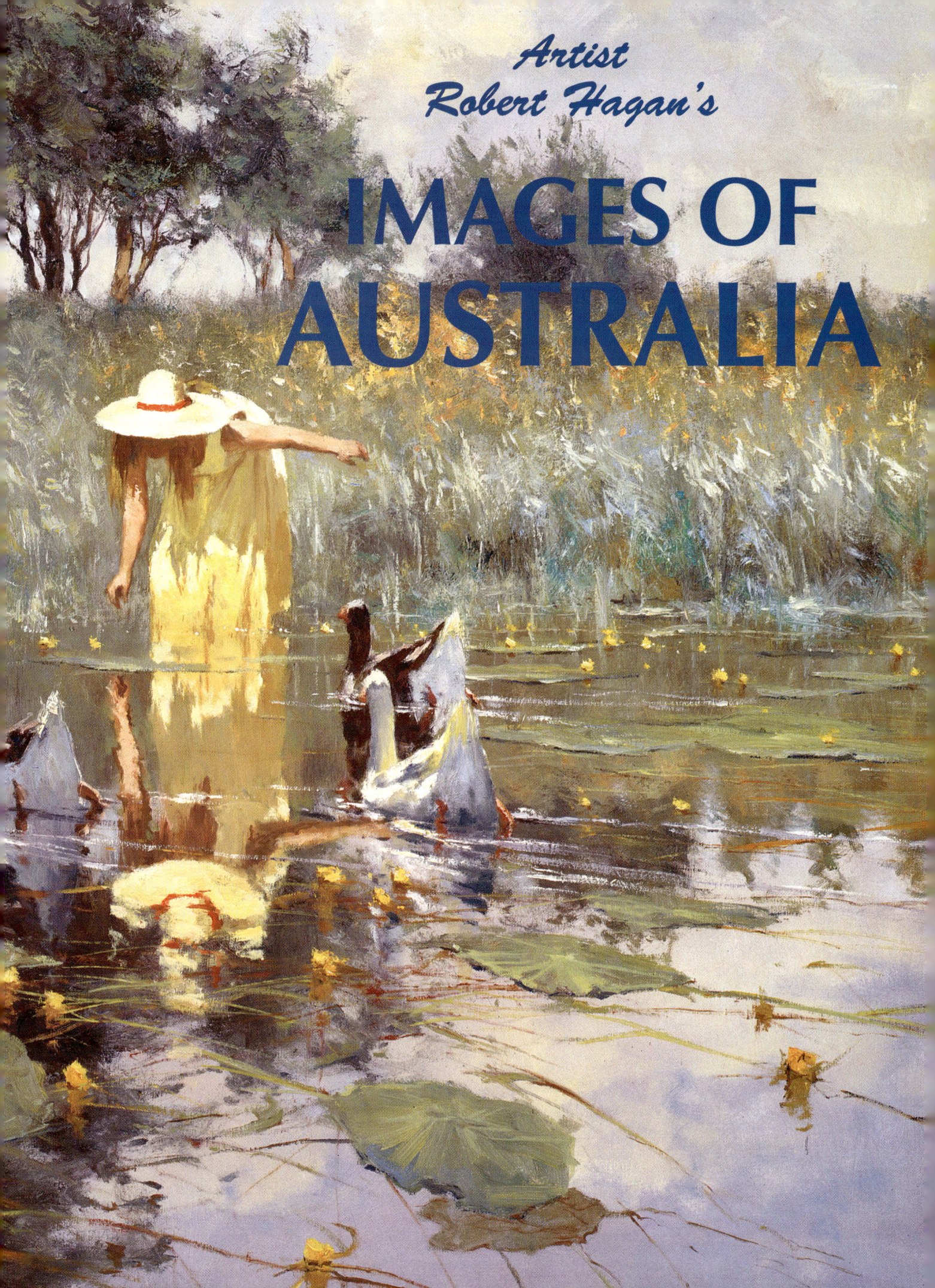

**This book is dedicated to my parents,
Evelyn and Len Hagan**

Frontis Art: Kookaburra II, The Enchanting Pond, and Sofala

NATIONAL LIBRARY OF CANADA
CATALOGUING-IN-PUBLICATION DATA

Hagan, Robert
Artist Robert Hagan's Images of Australia.

ISBN 0-9698515

Copyright © 1994 by Robert Hagan

All rights reserved. No portion of this publication may be reproduced, stored in a retrieval system, or transmitted in any form, or by any means, electronic ,mechanical, photocopying, recording, or otherwise, without the prior written permission of the publisher.

Published by:
IAS International Art Services Ltd.
Box HM 267
Hamilton, Bermuda
HM AX

Distributed in Australia by:
National Book Distributors and Publishers
Unit 3/2 Aquatic Drive
French's Forest, N.S.W. 2086
Australia

This book has been designed and typeset by ColorType, San Diego, CA, U.S.A.
Printed in Singapore by Kyodo Printing Co. (S'pore) Pte Ltd.

CONTENTS

INTRODUCTION   8

GONE FISHIN' WITH TRIGGER   11
CROSSING THE BULLOO   12–13
BILLINUDGEL   14–15
BOONAH FARMHOUSE   16–17
CHILLINGHAM ADVENTURERS   18–19
SISTERS   20–21
THE BRIDGE   22–23
THE COUNTRY MEETING   24–25
HAWKESBURY HUCKLEBERRIES   26–27
SAFE HARBOUR   28–29
THE GUN AT COOLAH   30–31
TRACKHOME   32–33
SECLUSIONS   34–35
TERRIGAL PELICANS   36–37
KELLY COUNTRY   38–39
OVENS IN FLOOD   40–41
BERNIE BOY   42–43
THE YABBIE CATCHER   44–45
THE MURRAY QUEEN   46–47
BALLARAT GIRLS   48–49
DUCK SHUFFLE   50–51
CUNNAMULLA SHEEP DOGS   52

THE OLD SEEDPLANTER   53
MOMENT OF AUTHORITY   54–55
FIVE DAY CREEK   56–57
STOCKMEN'S TEA BREAK   58–59
MURRAY BRIDGE ANGLING CLUB   60–61
PICNIC AT OAKBANK   62–63
AROONA VALLEY   64–65
SOFALA   66–67
FLASH OF COLOUR   68–69
THE CLYDES   70–71
SKEWBALD'S TIME OUT   72–73
THE TOWN GOES WILD   74–76
THE OPENING BATSMAN   76–77
REFLECTIONS ON THE SWAN   78–79
THE EXPLORERS   80–81
SPIRIT OF AUSTRALIA   82–83
THE YOUNG EXPLORER   84–85
GRASSHOPPER JOE   86–87
RESTOVER   88–89
SMALL DISAGREEMENTS   90–91
LAKE GEORGE IBISES   92–93
INDEX   94

INTRODUCTION
ROBERT HAGAN – Australian artist

If I can correctly remember the opening lines of J.D. Salinger's classic novel Catcher In The Rye it went something like, "If you really want to hear about it the first thing you'll want to know is where I was born and what my lousy childhood was like."

That's probably the main reason I was never quite in tune with Catcher In The Rye because the word "lousy" could hardly be applied to my own childhood. I was born in a most idyllic setting, a gloriously beautiful subtropical valley of the Tweed River on the far north coast of northern New South Wales and I had just about the most carefree and wonderful childhood imaginable.

With that scenario in mind, I can't possibly expect that anyone reading this book and musing over the photographic reproductions of my paintings will feel compelled to go out and shoot a famous rock star, as tragically occurred in the case of Catcher In The Rye. Well, anyway, I sure hope not!

Sigmund Freud's theories concerning the importance of childhood influences on later life seem to be clearly confirmed in my case. Most of my paintings are obviously influenced by my early memories and personal grateful appreciation of growing up in a warn, contented atmosphere in such a hauntingly beautiful area of Australia. So now, to paraphrase Mr. Salinger, if you really want to hear about it the first thing you'll want to know is where I was born and what my marvellous childhood was like.

Well, I was born in Murwillumbah on the north coast of New South Wales and from age eight I grew up in a nearby little town called Chillingham, just a few kilometres to the south of Byron Bay, the section of Australia often referred to with undeniable justification as God's Own Country. My mother Evelyn was and is a gracious, caring, committed, loyal and ever forgiving parent. My father, Len, an early renegade from the 'Big Smoke' as Sydney used to be called, was and is a man of considerable generosity and intellect. And even though he had to deal with me as both a father and as my first schoolteacher we have always been great pals.

I have a very sharp image of being about five years of age and living in nearby Brunswick Heads, also close to Murwillumbah, and wading in the shallows of the crystal clear Brunswick River with my mother and one of her closest girlfriends, both with their skirts tucked up and wearing colourful wide-brimmed straw hats to protect them from the Summer sun. They were both fishing with hand lines and were catching silver whiting every time they cast out on the shimmering waters. I was all the time under the almost tangible umbrella of their security and affection while blissfully splashing around by the water's edge and thoroughly enjoying the sights, sounds and smells of this marvellous natural playground. For me it was pure paradise.

My father's transfer to the school at Chillingham three years later meant even an improvement on paradise in my childlike view. And many years later, after all my world travelling, I still haven't come across any place that I would consider to be a better spot on this planet for a child to be raised. My years there, from age eight to sixteen, were absolutely magical.

Chillingham remains to this day a sleepy hollow, couched deeply in the upper and more remote valleys of the Tweed River. It supports no more than sixty or so residents, just as it did in my time there from the mid-1950s to the mid '60s with perhaps so-called transients accounting for about forty percent of the population. Transients was the label given to people who had only recently moved into the district — that is, they'd moved there sometime within the previous twenty or thirty years. The hamlet of Chillingham consisted of a butcher's shop, a general store, a trucking business, a sawmill, a School of Arts and the two-roomed Elementary school where my dear old Dad was the schoolmaster. And that was the lot.

In the morning and afternoon this remote little settlement was bathed in blue-purple shadows cast by the steep surrounding hills. Late afternoon thunderstorms in the summer months encouraged the lush, rainforest vegetation that blanketed any hillsides not already cultivated with the most luscious-tasting bananas this country could grow. Foliage was evergreen and broadleafed. Mountain parakeets of torquoise, scarlet and vivid yellow were always criss-crossing in the skies while both spotted and striped varieties of finches darted among the thornbushes and quail and wild turkey foraged in the undergrowth. Around the red-banked rivers occasional downward lightning flashes of iridescent blue signalled the presence of the kingfisher birds diving for baitfish.

Immediately to the south of the village, rising to a height of 3,600 feet was the towering Mount Warning, the long extinct volcano which presented an enormously dramatic backdrop for such a simple and uncomplicated little village. As television-crazy children we were always grateful to Mount Warning, because being more than 160 km from the nearest TV transmitting station in Brisbane, reception would normally be either unacceptably snowy or nonexistent. But thanks to a lucky angle on Mount Warning's rock face we were able to receive a perfect image on our TV screen via the judiciously positioned and upturned garden rake in the back yard. With the help of Mount Warning and the garden rake my childhood years were thus not deprived of the dubious enrichment of 77 Sunset Strip, Gunsmoke and all the other TV shoot-em-ups.

Again confirming Freud's claims, I would say that almost all of my paintings, in some nebulous way, directly relate to experience or recol-lections of events and images in and around Chillingham all those years ago.

Educationally, since I was the schoolmaster's son, there was little latitude for error or misdemeanour. I was generally bored with the regimen of elementary school, but I vividly recall admiring my teacher's (Dad) deliberate, yet effortless strokework when drawing trees and houses on the blackboard, with great instructive emphasis given to where light falls and where shadows are cast and the shapes that are thereby created.

During this time I remember my oldest brother David, while on vacation from college, wandering off into the bush and returning home hours later with a painting, done in water colours, of a nearby waterfall. This was the first painting I believe I had ever seen. It still haunts my mind as a wonderful painting. It was a slice of nature, chosen not according to any well-drilled scholastic principle but simply through natural artistic preference, a lovely uncomplicated contemplation of nature.

To my family's astonishment I belatedly picked up the learning bug and shot up from second last in class to second in the final examinations at Year 12. Then, more astonishingly, I went on to win a government scholarship to Newcastle University, majoring in economics and geography when I graduated in 1969 with a B.A. in Economics, and later a Post Grad. Diploma in Education.

After leaving university, I followed in father's footsteps, as the saying goes, and took up teaching, eventually being accepted for the master's position in economics at one of Sydney's most notable private schools. But even on the very day I started teaching at the new school I decided that my ultimate goal was to become a full time artist. I knew right from the start exactly what I wanted to paint — the special, out of the way places of my own country, Australia. So, in 1977, just when I could have settled myself into the relative security of a teacher's life, I did something that many wiser Australians have done before me over the last couple hundred years — I went walkabout.

I severed all my teaching connections and set off on foot to roam around Australia, grabbing any kind of odd job I could pick up — rouseabout in a shearing shed, woodchopping, track laying for outback railway lines, and in one wild outback Queensland town called Barcaldine I found myself selling tickets for Tex Morton's Travelling Wild West Show. I went walkabout for three years and in all that time I purposely never even did a sketch of anything. This was my observing period, building up a bank of never-forgotten Australian bushlife images.

The rest, as the cliche goes, is history. After several joint exhibitions of my paintings in Sydney I held my first solo exhibition at the Hunter-Taylor Gallery in the Sydney Hilton in 1984 and things have been pretty hectic ever since. In 1985 I felt a need to get far away from the associated madness of success in the art world, so I moved my entire studio to Thailand. I really didn't do all that much painting over there, but the trip was to change the course of my life. After three years I moved my highly mobile easel to another tropical paradise — the Phillippines.

Always a lover of German food, I happened to come across a German restaurant that not only served superb snitzels and cabbage roll dishes, but also went to the trouble of installing air conditioning. I was hooked on the place immediately, even more so after I'd been introduced to Emma, the manageress, with a smile that epitomized all the warmth and friendliness of the Phillippines. Needless to say, Emma soon became my wife and together we have three children who feature frequently in my paintings.

In the years since my temporary move to the Philippines I have established studios in England and the United States, apart from my permanent Australian base at Harbord in Sydney. I became deeply involved in painting the America's Cup yachts after Australia II's historic win in 1983 and currently I'm based in San Diego, USA, where the cup racing has continued to be decided since Australia's unsuccessful defence of the so-called Auld Mug in 1987.

For me, as an artist, the United States has been like a slowly awakening giant. Although I spent some time there in the early 1980s, only recently has its multi-faceted spell engulfed me and I'm about to embark on an American version of my earlier odyssey when I set out to paint images of Australia. In this book, the paintings are reflections of Australia the way I have seen it—a personal view, totally devoid of any outside stylised influences. In other words, it's the way I believe all Australians see, and remember, very personal magic moments and glorious scenes in their travels through this spectacularly beautiful country of ours.

GONE FISHIN' WITH TRIGGER
(Byron Bay, NSW)

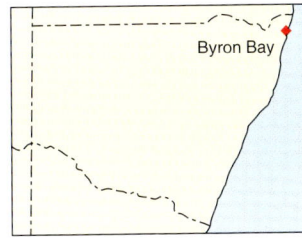

There's a fishing spot called Black Rock on a stretch of beach about halfway between Brunswick Heads and Byron Bay on the far north coast of New South Wales, and this is where you can see the sun come up before anyone else in Australia.

Black Rock is about the most easterly spot to go fishing in this country unless you want to dangle a line off the lighthouse at Cape Byron a few kilometres to the south. It was a hot summer's day, but if you look hard enough through the heat haze you'll see the mass of black rock by the water's edge that gave its name to this place. Up in the front, that's Lennie, one of the local Brunswick Heads fishermen, with his scruffy little mutt Trigger keeping him company.

It's getting near noon and it's up in the high thirties and the fish have stopped biting, so I reckon Lennie would probably be thinking it's about time he headed back into the Brunswick Heads pub for a cool cleansing ale. If he gets a move on he might make it in time to put a bet on the first race at Doomben. Profound ponderations on a not-so-bad day at Black Rock.

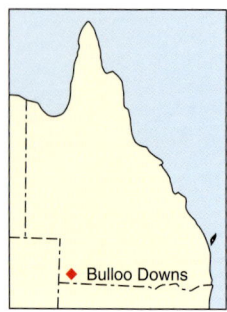

CROSSING THE BULLOO

(Near Bulloo Downs, Qld)

The Bulloo River in the south-west corner of Queensland can get dangerously dry in bad years until in some parts it's not much more than a pathetic trickle. But when there's water anywhere in the Bulloo Downs area in the middle of a drought it's the wearying job of the stockman to find it and head the cattle there. The rainfall at Bulloo Downs is always pretty low and for most of the year it's an arid and parched region. There's a town called Thargomindah on the Bulloo Downs — even pronouncing its name is enough to make the tongue go dry. Dry, it was not, however, the day this scene was captured.

BILLINUDGEL
(Far North Coast, NSW)

'There are eight million stories in the naked city,' they used to say on television, but if we use population as a criterion, there probably wouldn't be more than half-a-dozen stories in Billinudgel.

If you drive along the Pacific Highway on the far north coast of New South Wales, you'll eventually come to Billinudgel, but don't blink more than once when you get to it, or you'll miss the place altogether. I suppose there must be smaller towns in Australia, but not too many of them.

Billinudgel consists of just two main buildings and a few scattered houses. Naturally, one of the town's two buildings is a pub. This pub was famous in the hotel trade all over Australia because it was run by the country's oldest publican, the late Ma Ring. She was more than one hundred when she died and she was running the pub right to the end.

Ma Ring was quite a character. I remember going into her pub when she was in her late nineties. When she came into the bar, she looked around suspiciously, then pointed threateningly at one of the drinkers, 'You,' she yelled, 'get out, you're barred.' The bloke looked shocked. 'But I haven't had a drink in here for twenty-five years,' he protested. 'That's right,' said Ma Ring, 'and the last time you were in here I barred you for life. Now get out!'

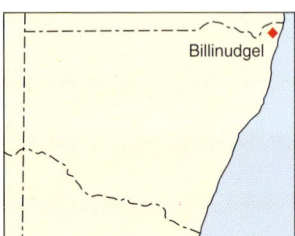

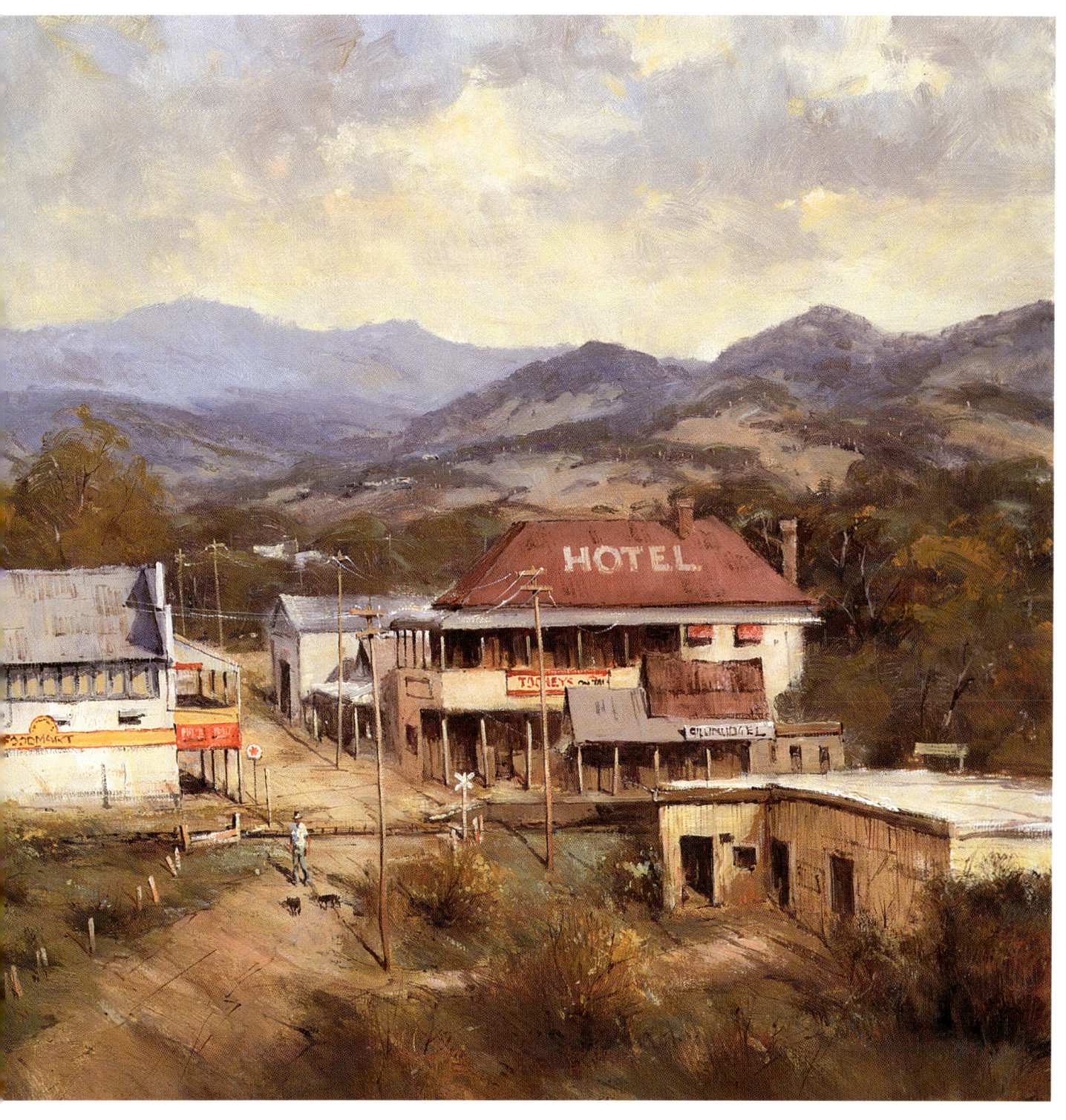

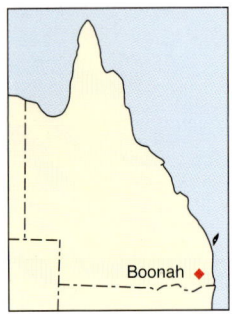

BOONAH FARMHOUSE
(Boonah, south-west of Brisbane, Qld)

When holidaymakers from the southern States of Australia visit Queensland one of the first things they notice is that most of the old farmhouses are built on stilts. Over the years I've heard some rather bizarre theories about the reason for the stilts.

Surprisingly, many southern Staters are convinced that the stilts are there to keep out the several varieties of deadly snakes and spiders found in Queensland. I could never understand the logic for this school of thought because in my experience in the bush, if an enterprising snake or spider is determined to get into the house, a few feet of stilts won't present any serious handicap.

The stilts, of course, come in very handy in times of flooding but the main purpose is merely to help keep the house cooler. When old farmhouses such as this one at Boonah were built, around the turn of the century, there was no such invention as air conditioning.

Boonah is a small town about 90 kilometres south-west of Brisbane with a population of around 2000. It's an historic town, originally a stopping place for bullock teams on the Sydney to Moreton Bay route. It was also the scene of many violent clashes between the early settlers and the Aborigines.

Like most other country towns the exodus of youth to the bright city lights is a sight that disappoints many older farm folk.

CHILLINGHAM ADVENTURERS

(Chillingham, north-east coast of NSW)

The scenery of this particular painting probably looks little different from the way it is at hundreds of other coastal inlets all around Australia, but it's a very personal and very special scene for me. I only have to take one swift glance to recognise it as my old favourite yabbie-catching spot on the eastern bank of the Wilson River at Chillingham, the town where I spent my childhood years.

Even on a very localised map you have to strain your eyes to find Chillingham because there's still not much there apart from a gas station and an old general store — just about the same as it was when I was a carefree, barefoot kid wagging school to go yabbie-catching at every opportunity. But we've all got to come from somewhere and, well, that's where I happen to come from, for better or worse. As things have panned out I consider myself most fortunate that I happened to grow up in this very laid back and very Australian little countryside village.

Chillingham is just a few kilometres north and inland of Brunswick Heads on the far north coast of New South Wales, and all through my career as a painter I've been strongly influenced by my happy childhood memories of this truly beautiful sub-tropical area of Australia. Writers are supposed to be at their creative best when they have a profoundly personal knowledge of the subject they're dealing with, and in many respects the same theory applies to the painting art form. For my part, I certainly find there's considerably less effort involved in putting down on canvas a scene that's so deeply entrenched in my memory that I can effortlessly recall every single detail — the way the tall dry grass came right down to the water's edge, what the temperature was like that day and even the way the wind was blowing.

If you can clearly remember details like that then it all flows easily from the mind then through the arm and right into the brush, a direct extension of your personal mental picture.

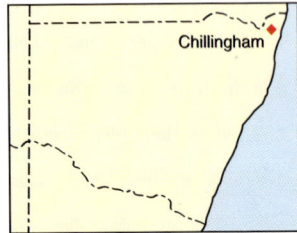

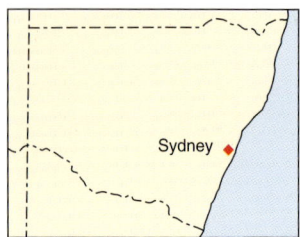

SISTERS

(Narrabeen Lakes area, Sydney, NSW)

As a landscape artist I've always tried to find out in advance some of the history of whatever area of land I have chosen to paint. I find this helps me to become more emotionally involved in the painting.

One fascinating story of early Australian history is associated with the Narrabeen Lakes area on the north-eastern side of Sydney. The lakes are named after a young Aboriginal girl called Narrabeen who lived here in the early 1830s. She was friendly with the Reynolds family who also lived in this area and was present when the Reynolds' home was attacked by a ferocious gang of bushrangers led by the notorious Big Mick. The bushrangers killed Mr. Reynolds, his wife, their baby, their fifteen-year-old son and two servants, but Narrabeen managed to escape. She ran all the way to the Parramatta settlement for help (a distance of some 45 kilometres), and guided soldiers back to the Reynolds' farmhouse where all the bushrangers were shot dead or captured.

It all happened about 150 years ago close to the very spot I have painted in this picture. It is strange that this place of such serene beauty could have any associations at all with one of the most brutally violent incidents of our colonial beginnings.

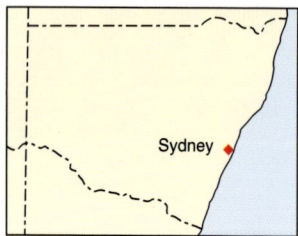

THE BRIDGE

(From Lavender Bay, Sydney, NSW)

The skyline of every major city in Australia seems to be changing almost overnight, but in Sydney, no matter how high in the clouds they construct new buildings, nothing stands out quite like the Sydney Harbour Bridge. I believe it will always be so. The bridge is the artistic focal point of the harbour and no modern painting of the harbour would be complete without some reference to it.

The bridge was painted battleship grey when it was built in 1932 and, as an artist, I'm happy that after all these years they've kept it the same colour. The grey is perfect for the bridge—it provides the quiet, peaceful backdrop to the multi-coloured pageant of all the yachts and merchant shipping, forever passing beneath the mighty span.

Around Sydney Harbour you can pick any one of a thousand places to paint the bridge, but my favourite place is here at Lavender Bay, on the bridge's western side. This view shows the Opera House, somehow made to seem rather insignificant under the towering domination of the mighty arch.

THE COUNTRY MEETING
(Chillagoe, NE Qld.)

In mid-May it starts to get a little bit chilly in all the southern States, but it's never chilly all-year-round in Chillagoe, a small bush town way up in the tropical north end of Queensland, about 150 km inland from Cairns.

Mid May, in fact, is just about the perfect time of the year to be in Chillagoe, because the Dry season is now well under way, so it's neither too hot nor too humid and, more importantly, it's also the time of the year they run their annual racemeeting. I don't know if these days they've gone all modernised with starting stalls or photo finish cameras, but when I attended a racemeeting at Chilligoe many years ago they had a track laid out with a winning post and a beer selling outlet — and that was about it. Nothing much else in the way of course facilities was considered of vital importance, so all they had to do was find horses and jockeys, a few bookmakers and an enormous supply of beer kegs and they considered themselves perfectly ready to stage a racemeeting.

I think it's fair to say that the general atmosphere at the annual Chilligoe races could properly be described as "laid back." To be quite truthful, it was just about the most laid back atmosphere I've ever seen at any kind of sporting meeting I've ever attended anywhere in the world.

By way of an example, as the clerk of course led the field out onto the track for the first race, I couldn't help noticing that he was occasionally slurping from a can of Fourex, which, of course, is the beer fervently favoured by all patriotic Queenslanders. As for the judge, perched precariously up there in a box on top of a terrifyingly fragile looking scaffolding — well it was bit hard to tell from where I was standing whether he had a can in hand as well! But at this laid back track, everyone had a can in hand, so why not the judge?

As it happens, I was told that just a few years earlier at one of these annual Chillagoe meetings that just as the horses were passing the post the judge had got himself so laid back he'd fallen head over heels backwards clean out of the judge's box and he'd landed flat on his rear end.

Not surprisingly, some sections of the crowd loudly accused the judge of being intoxicated, which of course he vehemently denies. But he was so upset by all this scurrilous questioning of his sobriety he felt an urgent need to repair to the nearest bar for a cold tinnie. A little later the clerk of the course joined the judge at the bar — he wanted another can in his hand while he led out the field for the next race.

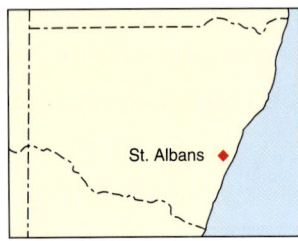

HAWKESBURY HUCKLEBERRIES

(Near St Albans, north-west of Sydney, NSW)

It's the late 1980s, but the scene could easily be from the early days of the Colony in the 1830s, as carefree children go fishing in the shallows of the historic Hawkesbury River, near St Albans, about 70 kilometres north-west of Sydney. In this secluded untouched part of the river the scenery hardly differs from the way it was when the first settlers came here with their children to build a cluster of homes set among small green paddocks. Many of those old homes are still there at St Albans and at the nearby older town of Windsor. The Settlers Arms, built in 1842, is the oldest inn in the St Albans area, surviving countless bushfires and floods over the last one-and-a-half centuries.

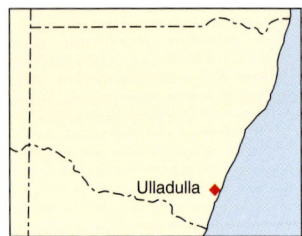

SAFE HARBOUR

(Ulladulla, South Coast, NSW)

'Ulladulla' isn't the prettiest name in the world for a town. But as Shakespeare said, what's in a name? And indeed, Ulladulla happens to be one of the most beautiful fishing villages on the New South Wales southern coastline. It's also a holiday resort and is located off the Princes Highway about 230 kilometres by road south of Sydney.

The day I painted this tranquil scene there was barely a breath of wind and only the suggestion of a ripple on the water, lapping gently at the sides of the boats tied up by the jetty. The locals told me it can be like that in the sheltered waters at Ulladulla even when there's a fearsome southerly buster blowing just outside. A storm-battered yacht in the Sydney to Hobart race has often limped gratefully into the safety of Ulladulla, seeking sanctuary from a raging Pacific Ocean. The name 'Ulladulla' actually comes from an Aboriginal word meaning 'a safe harbour,' so the town is very aptly named after all.

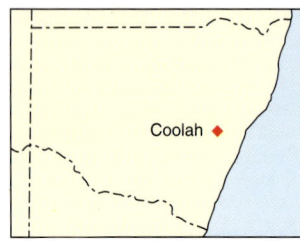

THE GUN AT COOLAH

(Coolah, north-western NSW)

The best shearer in any shed, in sheep shearing terminology, is called 'The Gun.' This title means he can consistently shear 200 or more sheep in a single day.

In this painting 'The Gun' is the perspiring, broad-shouldered-singleted shearer in the foreground who is bent over a supine merino that he has already half-shorn after only about two minutes.

The shearing is taking place in an old shed, built in the early 1920s as far as anyone can remember, and it's just outside a small town called Coolah in a sheep, cattle and wheat belt about 400 kilometres north-west of Sydney.

Sometimes when I look into a battered old weatherboard shearing shed like this one, the same kind of respectful feelings come over me as if I were peeking into a magnificent cathedral. I think it's because the solemn traditions of sheep shearing remind me in some way of the religious ritual of a church service. If you walk into a church or a sheep shearing shed you know exactly what you are going to witness. It's always the same, in their different ways.

TRACK HOME

(Near Swan Hill, VIC)

In these days of fully-mechanised, high-tech farm and station equipment it's most reassuring, at least from a nostalgic artist's point of view, that on some of the older properties the horse is still a vital part of the daily work routine and even the humble dray has not yet been entirely expunged from the Australian rural scene. Together, the workhorse and the dray make an irresistible painting subject.

I found this particular combination of horse and dray moving along a well-worn bush track close to Swan Hill in north-east Victoria. The track is very near the south bank of the Murray River and it was around about here that the explorers Burke and Wills crossed the Murray back in 1860 on their ill-fated attempt to traverse the continent from south to north.

But the history of Swan Hill goes back even further than Burke and Wills. The area was originally named by an earlier explorer, Thomas Mitchell, and he set up a camp on a sandy rise by the river. A lagoon on the other side of the sandy rise was heavily populated with black swans at the time that Mitchell camped overnight and apparently the swans didn't appreciate the visit by Mitchell and his entourage so they kept him awake all night with their constant squawking. If nothing else, Swan Hill is certainly rich in Australian historical trivia.

SECLUSIONS
(West of Cairns, Qld)

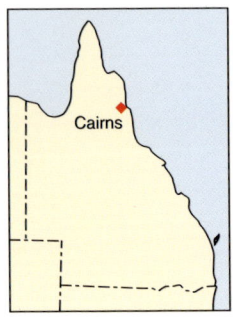

Most people tend to think of the Cairns district of far north Queensland in terms of big game fishing or sugar cane growing and, more recently, a tourism and recreational centre especially popular with the golfing fraternity. But if you go exploring inland a little bit, away from all the new high rise apartments and golf courses, it's still possible to come across secluded little billabongs such as this one.

Hopefully, this sublime little spot will be preserved for its own pristine beauty and not ignominiously transformed into a mere water hazard on a par-three hole, subjected to regular bombardments of wildly astray hook shots.

What an obscenity it would be for a splashing golf ball to shatter a private meditative moment of serenity in such a Garden of Eden setting as this.

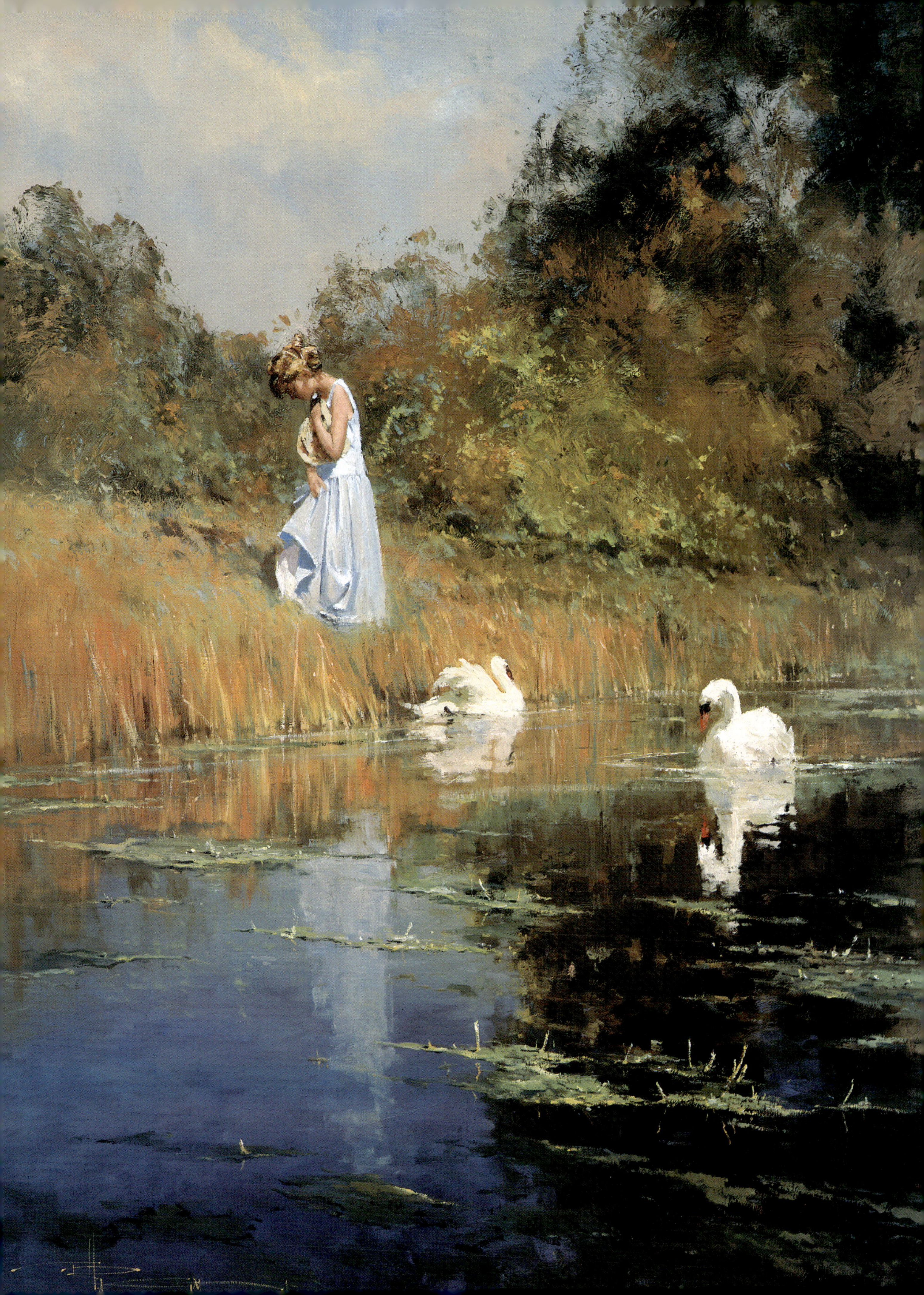

TERRIGAL PELICANS
(Terrigal NSW)

Soon after the end of World War Two when motor cars started to become affordable for the working man, Sydneysiders began looking for nearby holiday towns to escape the rat race for a weekend. Undoubtedly, one of the most popular getaway places for work-weary Sydneysiders to visit for a couple of days fishing or bushwalking was and still is Terrigal, a coastal holiday resort about 100 km drive up the Pacific Highway and just 11 km past Gosford.

Terrigal, I only recently discovered, gets its name from an Aboriginal word meaning "place of little birds," which surprised me greatly, because in my many visits here over the years I've always been struck by the unfailing presence of pelicans in vast numbers. These majestic feathery jumbo jets seem to avoid the Terrigal resort's very popular surfing beach, but you'll find large groups of them constantly hunting for fish feeds in the many secluded little inlets on either side of town.

The tranquil and idyllic inlet I've painted here is only about three kilometres from the now bustling shopping centre of Terrigal and it's typical of dozens of similar quiet and peaceful waterways in this area where pelicans are clearly the most visible and most dominant bird species. Presumably the pelicans have been hanging around here for thousands of years, so why, I wonder, did the Aborigines come up with such a classic misnomer as "Place Of Little Birds"?

I can only assume that some very dry-witted tribal elder way back in the Dreamtime must have had an ironic sense of humour.

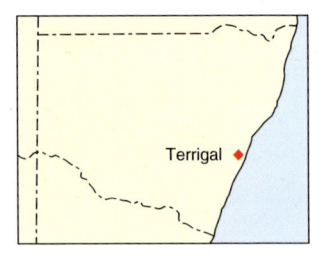

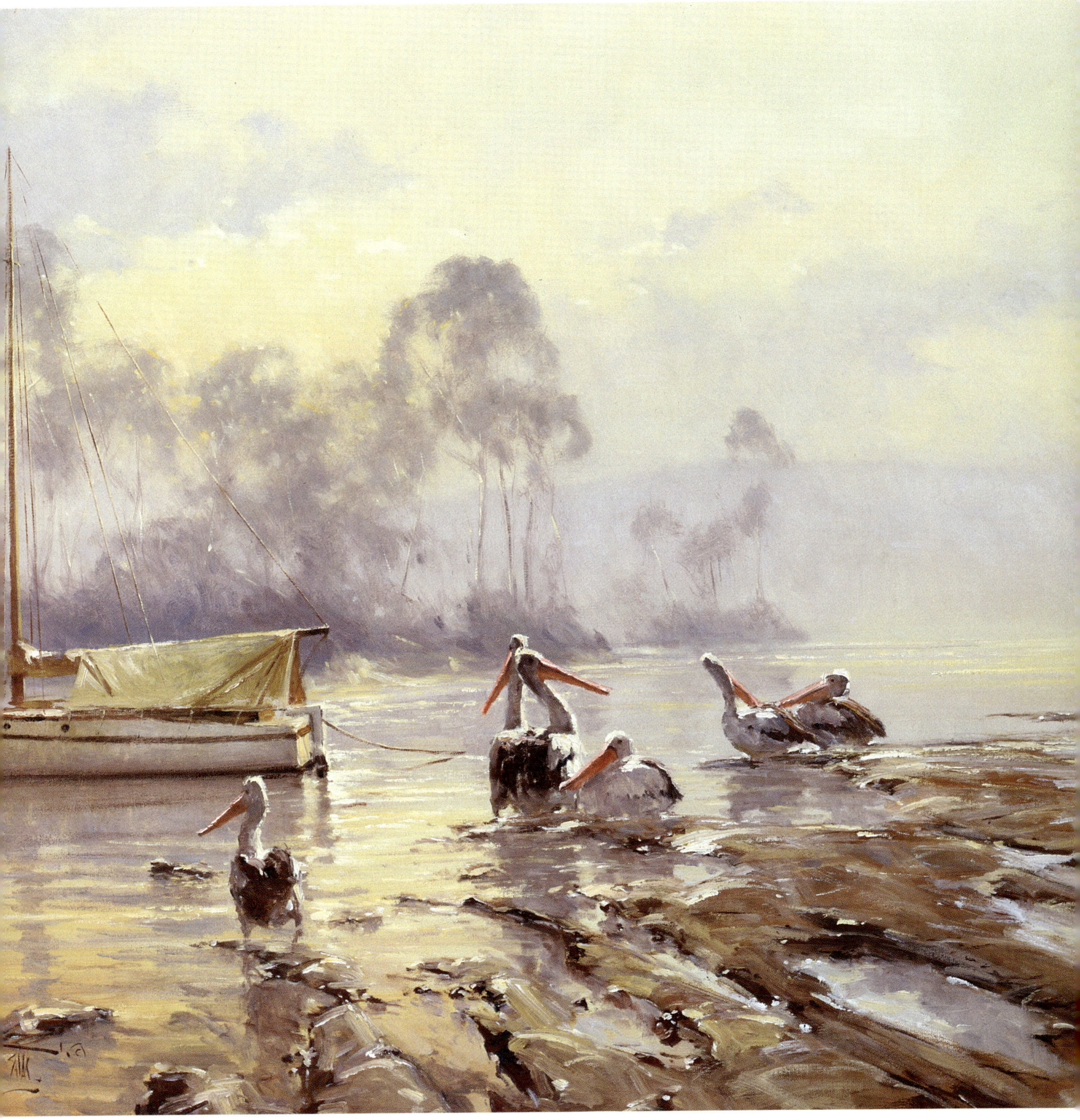

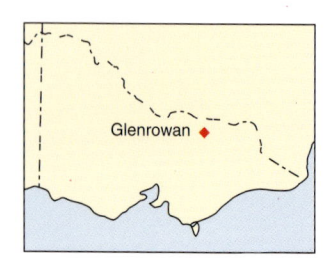

KELLY COUNTRY

(Near Glenrowan, Vic.)

A few kilometres away, on the other side of the hill in the background of this painting, lies the small but famous Victorian town of Glenrowan, where Ned Kelly and his gang made their last stand. In the foreground is a stream running off the Owens River and all around here is known by the locals as Kelly Country. Ned and his gang—Dan Kelly, Joe Byrne and Steve Hart—would doubtless have ridden close by here on their way to bank holdups back in their heyday of the late 1870s. Who knows, they might even have stopped at this very spot to give their horses a drink. An idle fancy perhaps, but when you're in Kelly Country the mind tends to wander and you can feel Ned's haunting presence everywhere.

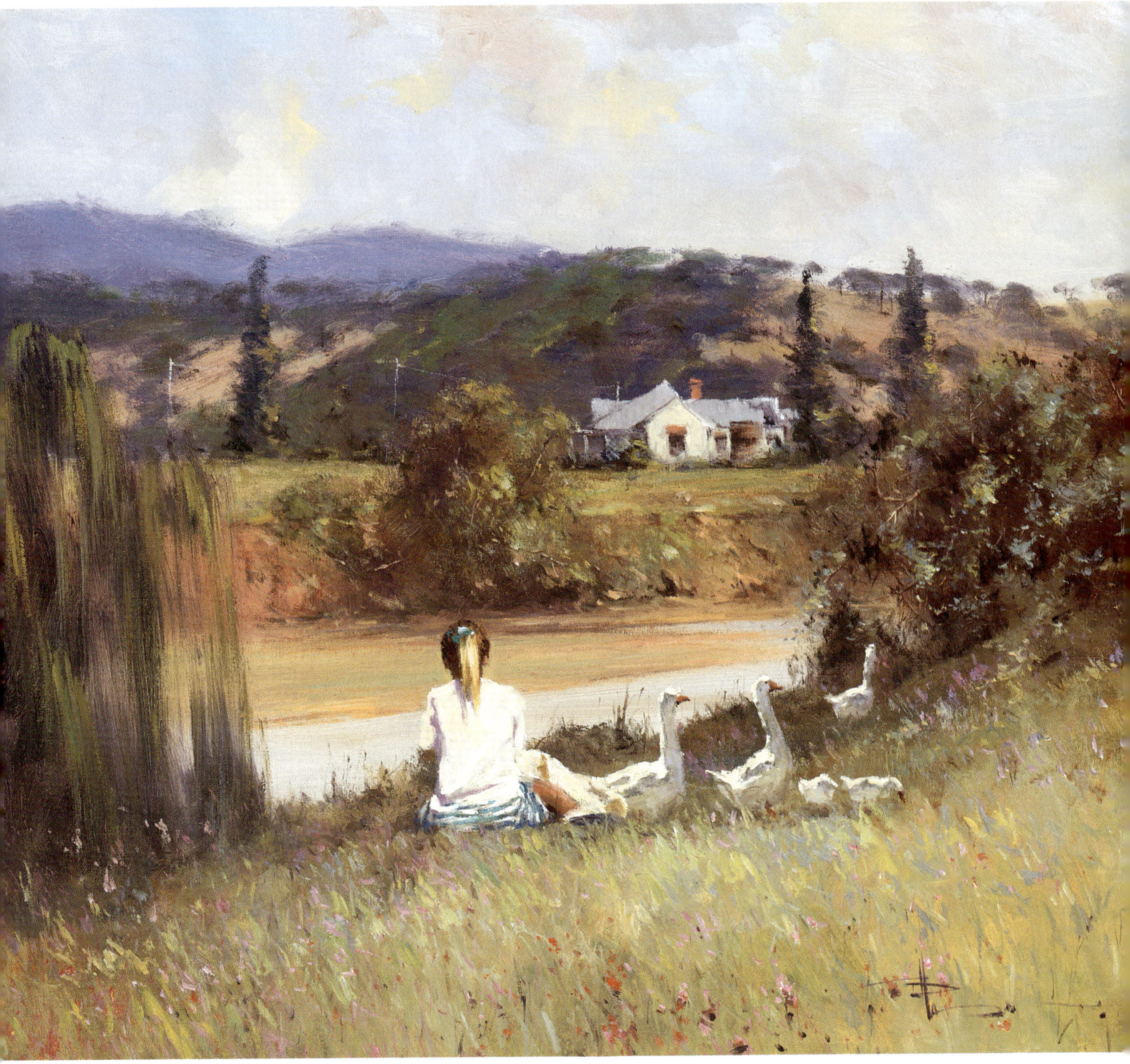

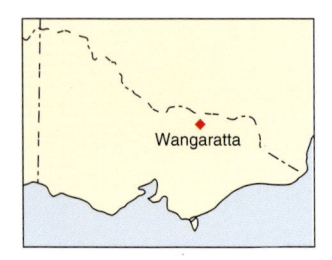

OVENS IN FLOOD

(Ovens River, near Wangaratta, Vic.)

The Ovens River in Victoria runs off the Murray River near the town of Corowa. It goes past the small town of Peechelba on its way to the larger town of Wangaratta. This painting shows a section of the Ovens just past Peechelba and on the edge of the Warby Range State Park, during a reasonably mild flood period.

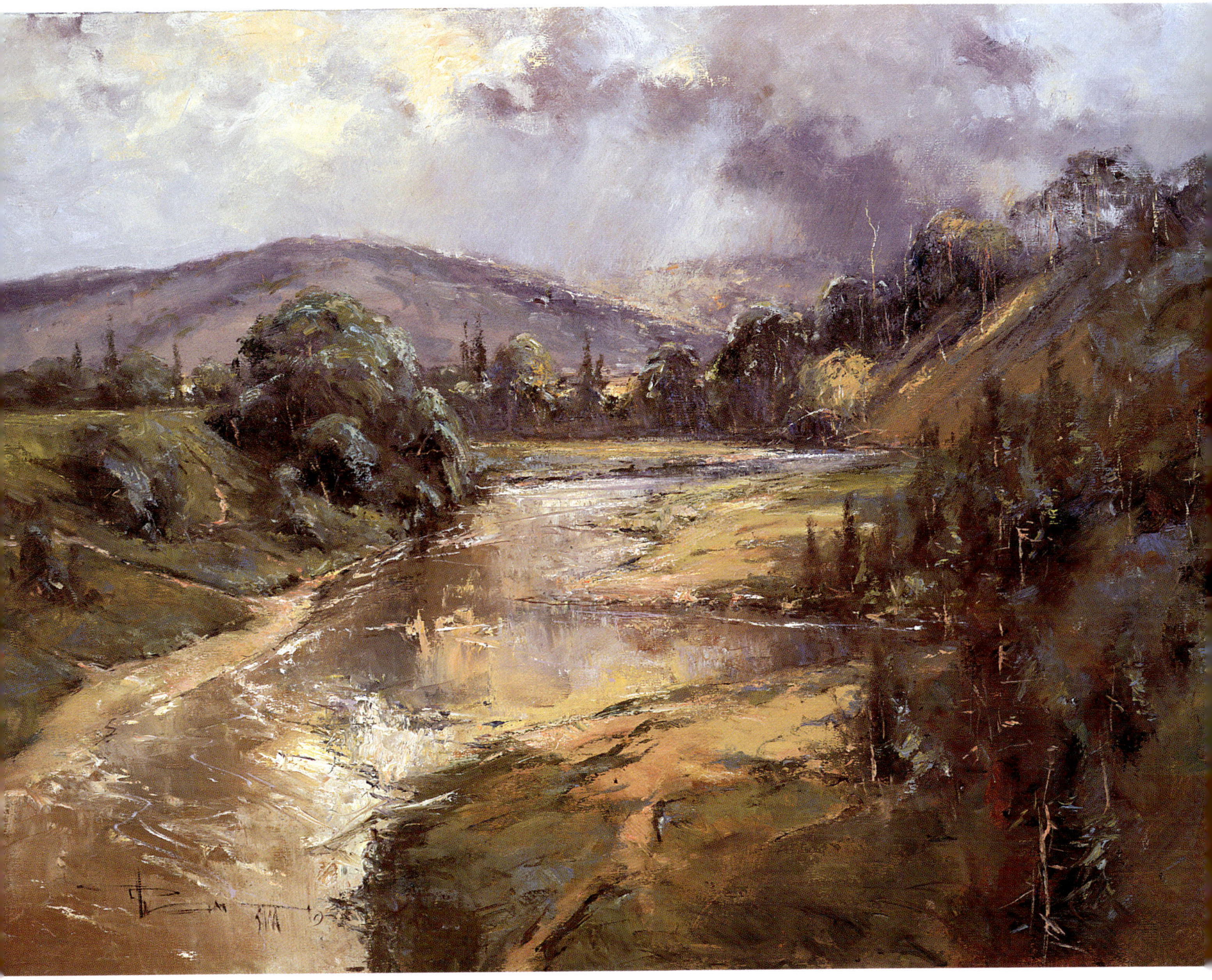

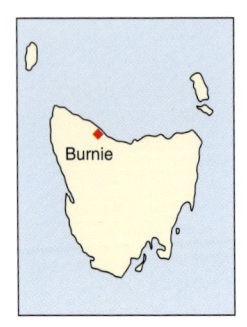

BURNIE BOY

(Burnie, Tas.)

Burnie is a particularly busy port town by the shores of Emu Bay on the north coast of Tasmania, directly facing Bass Strait. It is a well-developed deepwater port and natural harbour and is currently handling more than two million tonnes of cargo per year. The only bigger port in Tasmania is the capital city, Hobart. The little boy in this painting is Wayne, the son of a Burnie wharf laborer. Wayne's two burly uncles also work on the Burnie wharves and judging by the sturdy physique of young Wayne it would seem that one day he will be eminently qualified to follow the family profession.

43

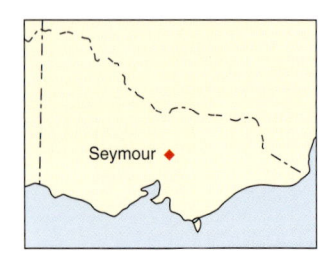

THE YABBIE CATCHER

(Near Seymour, Vic.)

One of the joys of growing up in the bush for thousands of Australian children is to go fishing for yabbies, small freshwater crustaceans that, for some reason, have never made an impact on the Australian menu even though they are relished by gourmets all over the world.

The young yabbie catcher in this painting is being carefully tutored in the finer skills of this intricate sport by his father on the banks of a stream running off the Goulburn River near Seymour, Victoria. The Puckapunyal Army Camp isn't far from here and no doubt over the years countless soldiers have snuck away from the camp to do a spot of yabbie catching to brighten up the Army diet.

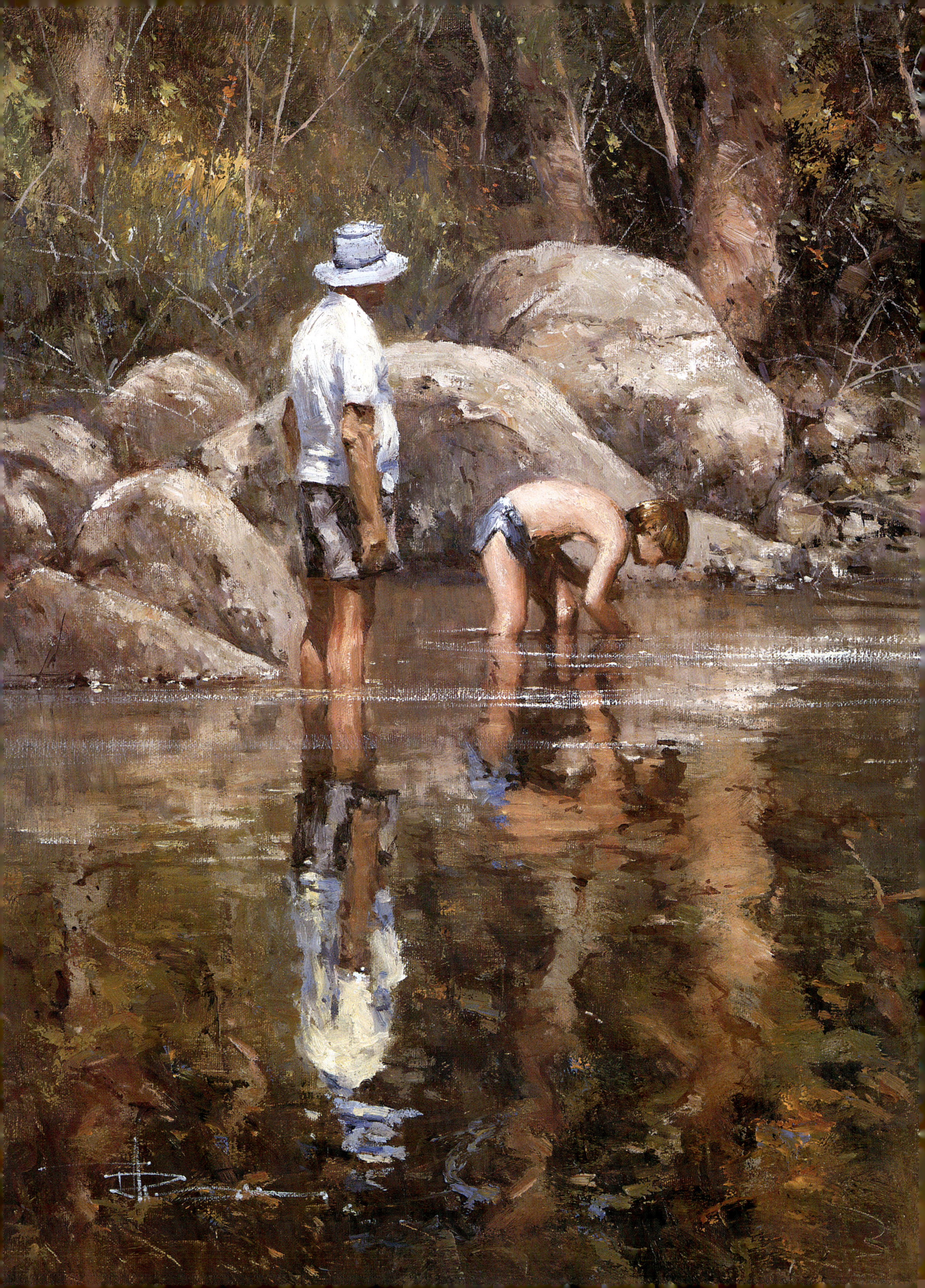

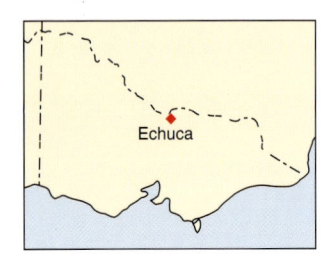

THE MURRAY QUEEN
(Echuca, Vic.)

Echuca is a small town in Victoria, on the south bank of the middle Murray River, associated with the romantic days of the old paddlewheel steamers.

In the 1880s Echuca was a booming port for riverboats such as the two relics in this painting. When the railways started to stretch through the Riverina area, however, both the river trade and the town of Echuca went into decline. Fortunately, in 1969 the National Trust declared the old port site a historic area and also listed many of the old buildings and structures, so Echuca started a new life as a tourist centre.

Modern paddlewheel boats now carry tourists on slow but restful cruises down the Mighty Murray, keeping the riverboat tradition alive. Some of the nineteenth century paddlewheel steamers have been restored as tourist attractions, but of course their working days are well and truly over. They just sit there at anchor, motionless reminders of a romantic era in Australian history.

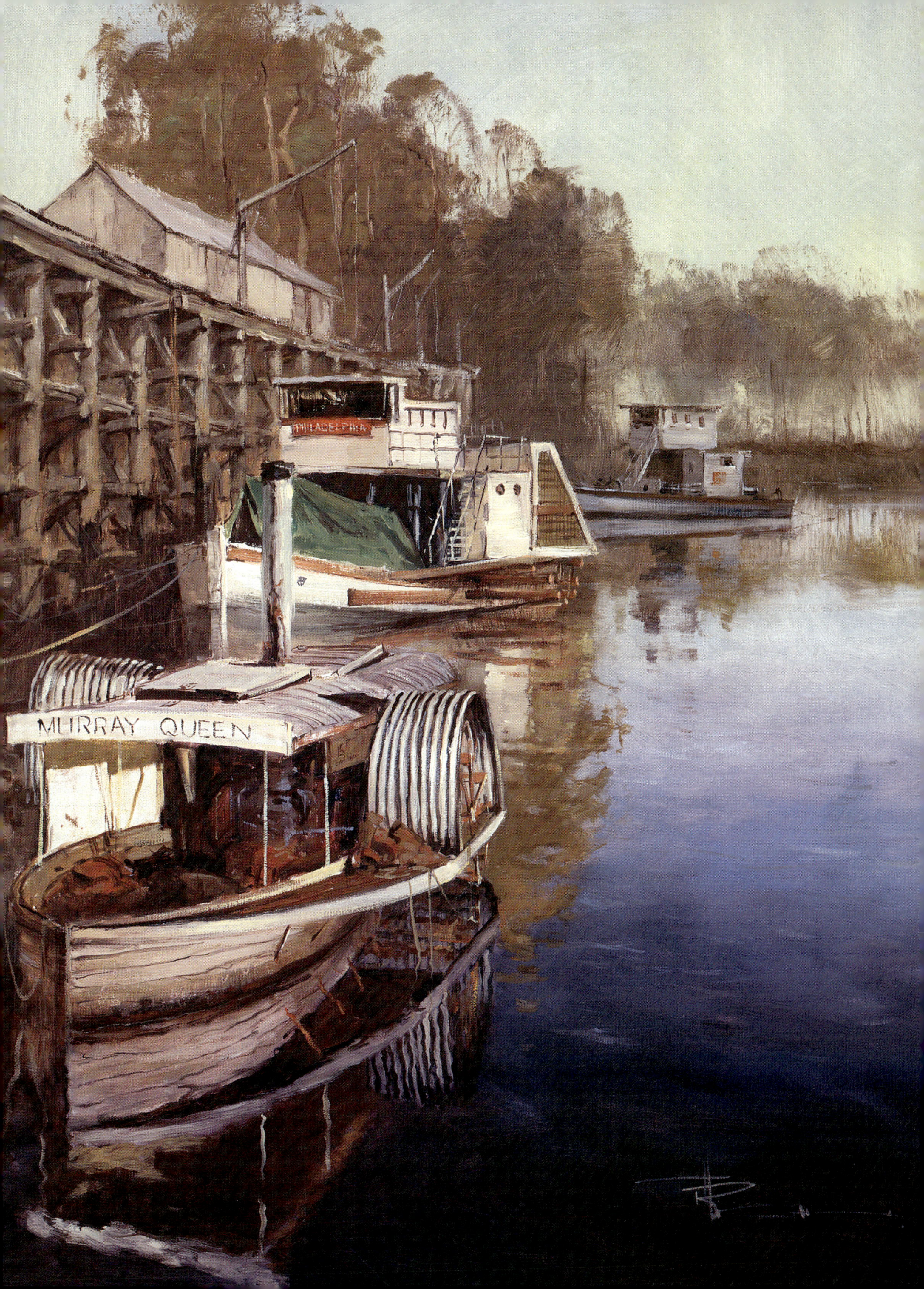
MURRAY QUEEN
PHILADELPHIA

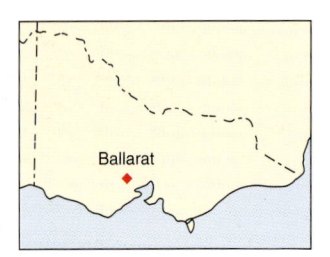

BALLARAT GIRLS
(Ballarat, Vic.)

The setting for this painting is a picnic spot on the banks of the Yarrowee River a few kilometres out of Ballarat, one of my favourite Victorian cities. Ballarat is a hustling, bustling city these days but in the bush outside the town there is still evidence of the gold rush days of the nineteenth century. If you potter around some of the long deserted goldfields near here, it's still possible to discover all kinds of abandoned equipment used by the miners even as far back as 1854 when Peter Lalor led the battle for the Eureka Stockade.

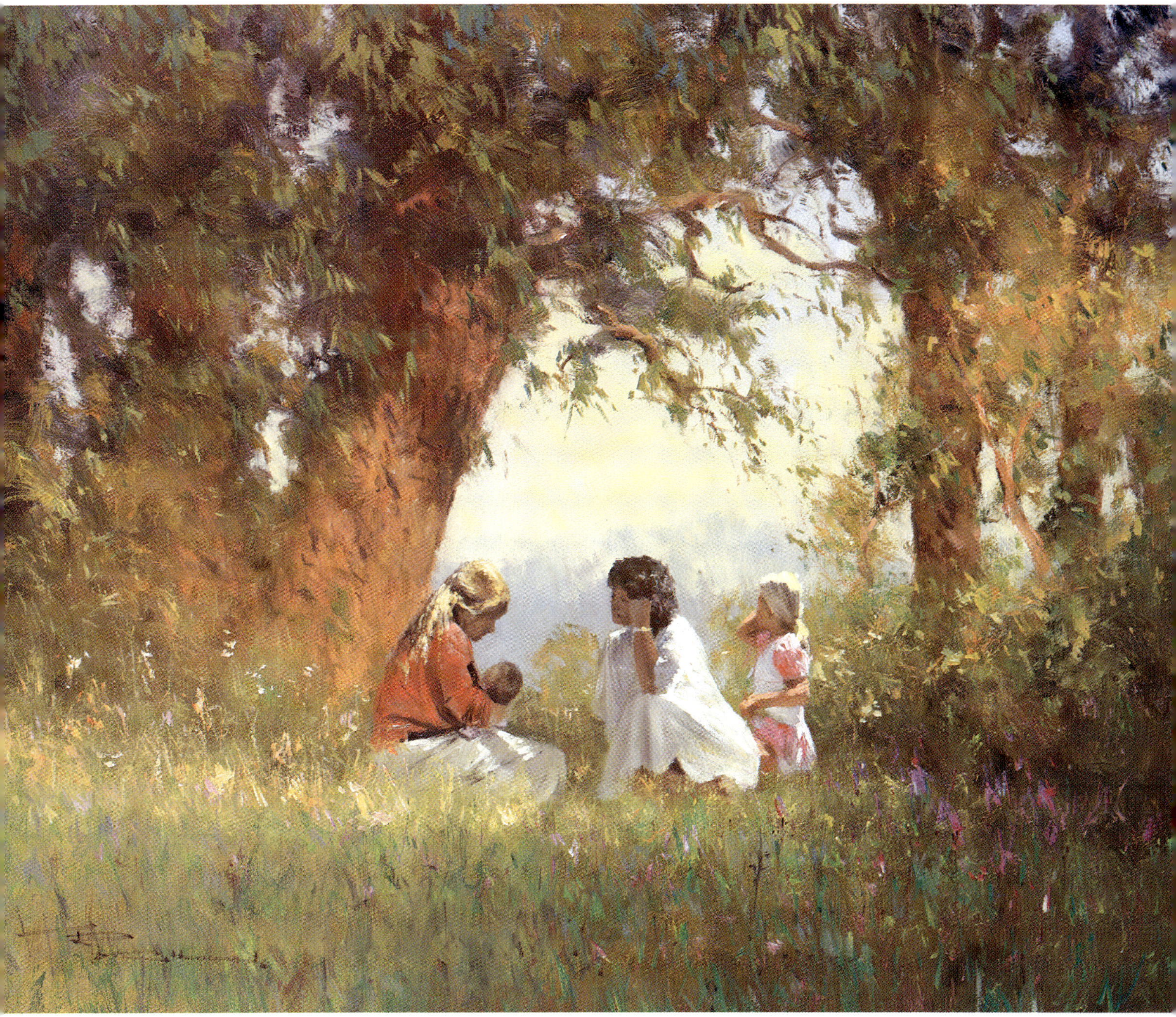

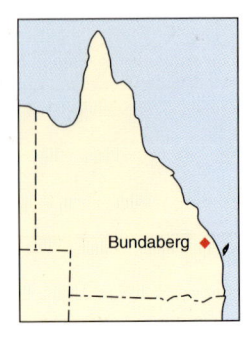

DUCK SHUFFLE

(Bundaberg, Qld.)

Whenever I get a bad cold I've always found that a hot toddy of Bundaberg Rum with honey and lemon juice makes me feel a heck of a lot better, even if it doesn't do much to cure the cold. Bundaberg is a coastal city in south-east Queensland and, I guess, it's main claim to fame is its long-established production of the distinctive tasting rum produced from the vast cane fields which dominant the landscape all around here.

But away from the canefields there are some rather beautiful little billabongs, like the one depicted here, alongside the Burnett River which flows on from this point into the city. Although it's been rum production that's put Bundaberg on the map, it's also well known to this country's historians as the birthplace of three famous Australians in quite different areas of achievement. The opera star Gladys Moncrieff was born here, as was the Test cricket wicketkeeper Don Tallon and aviator Bert Hinckler who made the first solo flight from England to Australia.

That historic flight took place in 1928 but seven years earlier Bert amazed the entire nation when he flew a light plane 1207 km from Sydney to his home town of Bundaberg non-stop and landed right there in the main street. Next time you pass through Bundaberg make sure you pause for a few moments and read about his remarkable aviation pioneering exploits engraved on no less than three very impressive Bert Hinckler Memorials. One of them is alongside the Burnett Bridge, not far from the scene in this painting, recording the fact that Bert once flew his aircraft right under the bridge to the ecstatic delight of the townsfolk who turned out en masse to watch him do it.

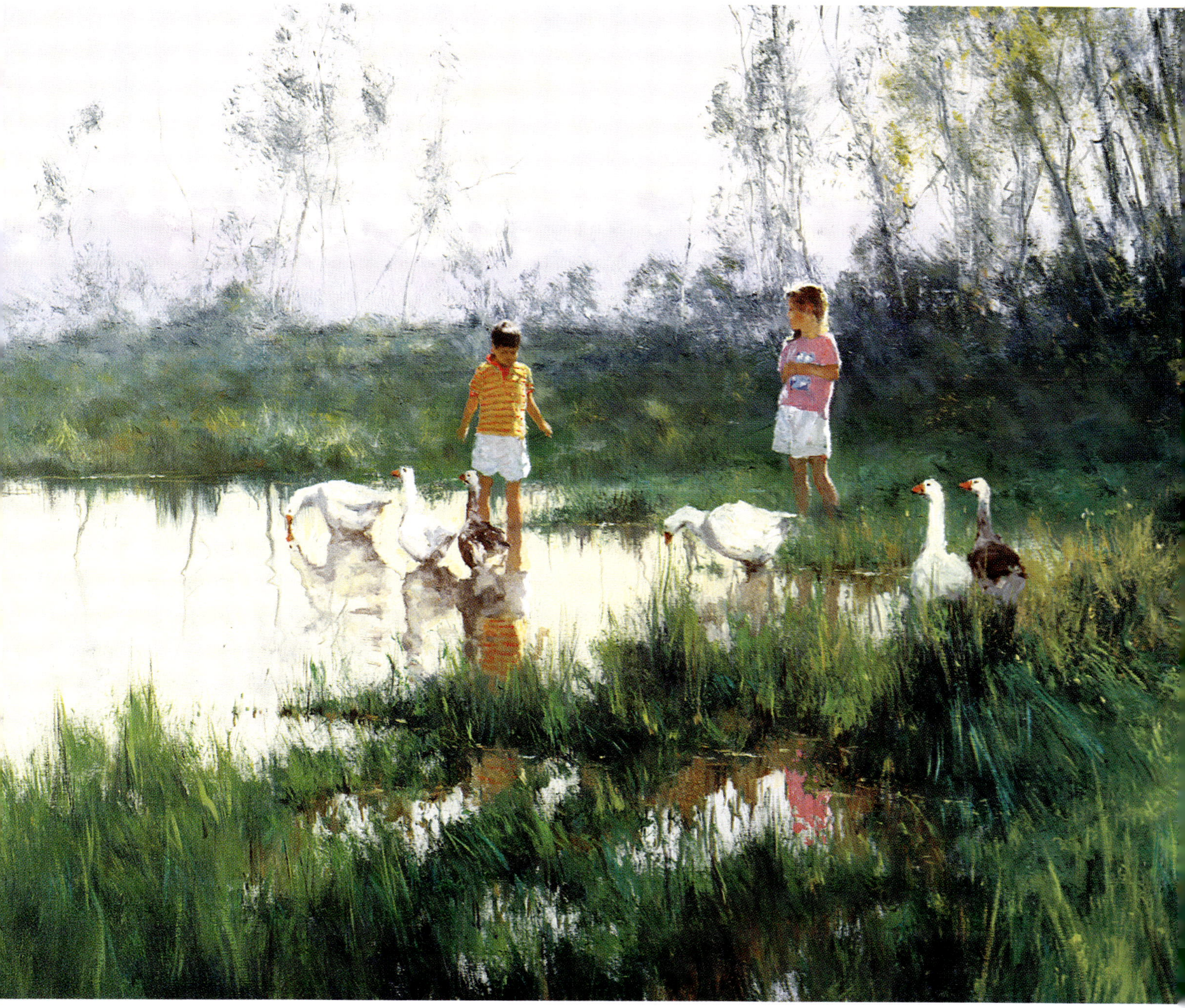

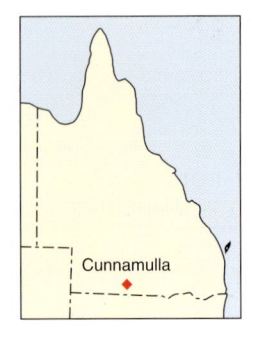

CUNNAMULLA SHEEP DOGS
(South-western Qld)

Wool growing is the main industry of the region around Cunnamulla in south-west Queensland and the sheep dogs who work here are as smart and as tough as those you would find in sheep country anywhere in Australia. These working dogs are all muscle and sinew and they're trained to work all day without a drink. I've been to Cunnamulla several times, but for some reason I've always forgotten to buy myself the famous local hat—a big broad-brimmed hat they call the 'Cunnamulla Cartwheel.'

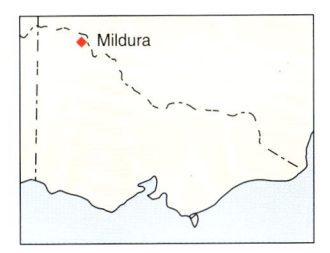

THE OLD SEEDPLANTER

(Near Mildura, Vic.)

This is a rather nostalgic scene from the Mallee district of north-western Victoria, not far from Mildura. I visited this area in my early twenties and I can remember seeing an old seedplanter being used by a farmer in the district. Somehow the picture of that nineteenth-century equipment seemed to stick in my mind when I decided to do a painting of the Mallee area. Today, of course, modern farming technology is used on the farmland outside Mildura, but this old seedplanter is a reminder of the slower pace of farm life in the old days. Australia the way things used to be.

MOMENT OF AUTHORITY
(West of Texas, Qld.)

Whenever I'm asked if I've ever visited Texas I can boastfully reply, "Which one? I've been to both." On my last visit to America I toured extensively all over the famous Lone Star State, but I'm also lucky enough to have spent some time in Australia's Texas, the dusty little cattle town, about 330 km by road south-west of Brisbane and just a few kilometres north of the border with New South Wales. Bit ridiculous making any kind of comparison between the two, but Australia's Texas is still quite a colourful little town and, just as it is with America's Texas, anyone born in the Aussie version can rightfully lay claim to the proud nickname "Tex" all their lives. As many of them do.

The town is in a sparsely habitated area of southern Queensland noted as a tobacco growing district and fine cattle country. Consequently it produces some of Australia's top drovers and rodeo riders.

I'm not exactly sure how Australia's Texas came by its name, but I would imagine that when the town was founded around the 1870s it would have looked pretty much like some of the Wild West settlements in the original Texas. And it certainly must have been quite a wild town in its early days because just about the first building erected was a police station and lock up, which has now been turned into a museum.

I was amused to learn that the nearest town to Texas is called Silver Spur and as names go, you sure can't get much more Wild West than that. Understandably, I suppose, it must be difficult for the local stockmen to resist being caught up in a transplanted American Wild West atmosphere and I noticed they tended to look just that little more like American cowboys than stockmen elsewhere in Australia.

This is a painting of two young stockmen rounding up stray cattle on the banks of the Dumaresque River, just a few kilometres west of Australia's Texas, but if these boys allowed their imaginations to wander a little they could easily be Butch Cassidy and The Sundance Kid making their getaway after robbing a bank in Dodge City.

And, if you grow up in a place called Texas, I suppose you'd occasionally make believe that the little river running through the town isn't the Dumaresque at all. It's really the mighty Rio Grande.

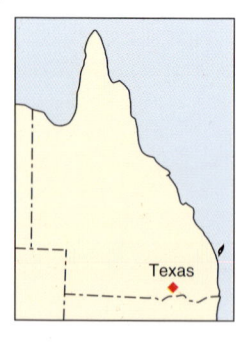

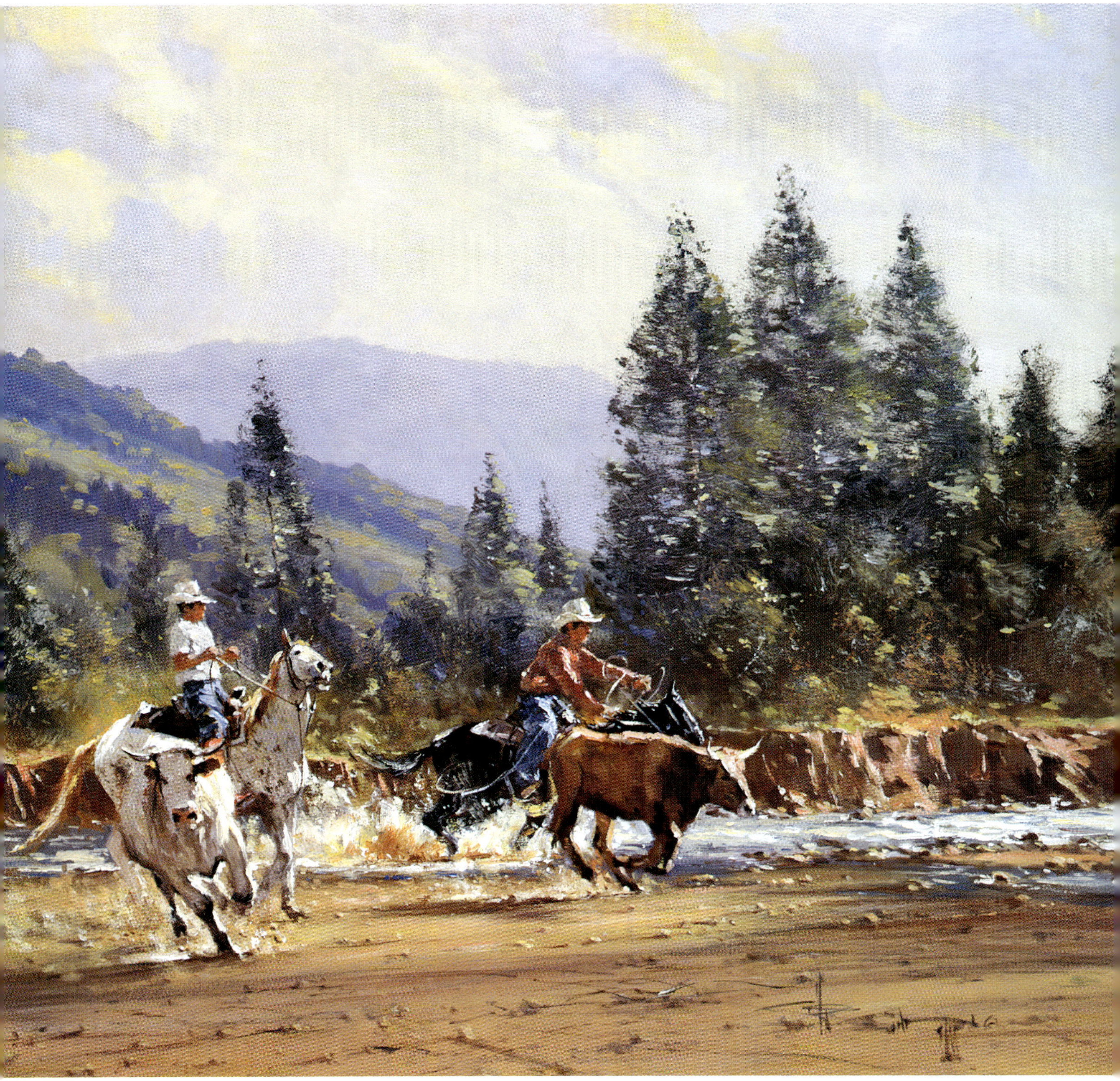

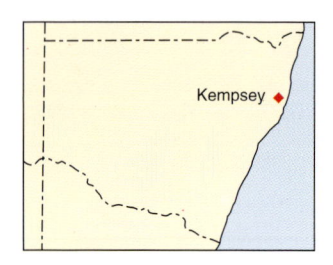

FIVE DAY CREEK

(near Kempsey, NWS)

The Macleay River runs through the northern NSW town of Kempsey and you'll find the intriguingly-named Five Day Creek trickling off the Macleay about 40 kilometres or so northwest of the township. The creek really was little more than a trickle of water only a few inches deep when I happened to come along with my brush and pallette at the end of a long dry summer, but apparently it can get quite deep and swollen when there's a bit of rain about.

The creek was named by the great explorer John Oxley who camped on the southern bank when he was exploring this area in 1818 and it must have presented an entirely different spectacle to Oxley than it did for me. Back then the rain had been coming down heavily and the creek would have looked more like a river in flood because Oxley and his men were very reluctant to have a crack at crossing it. They were stuck there for five very boring days before they'd felt the water level had receded enough to allow them to get across.

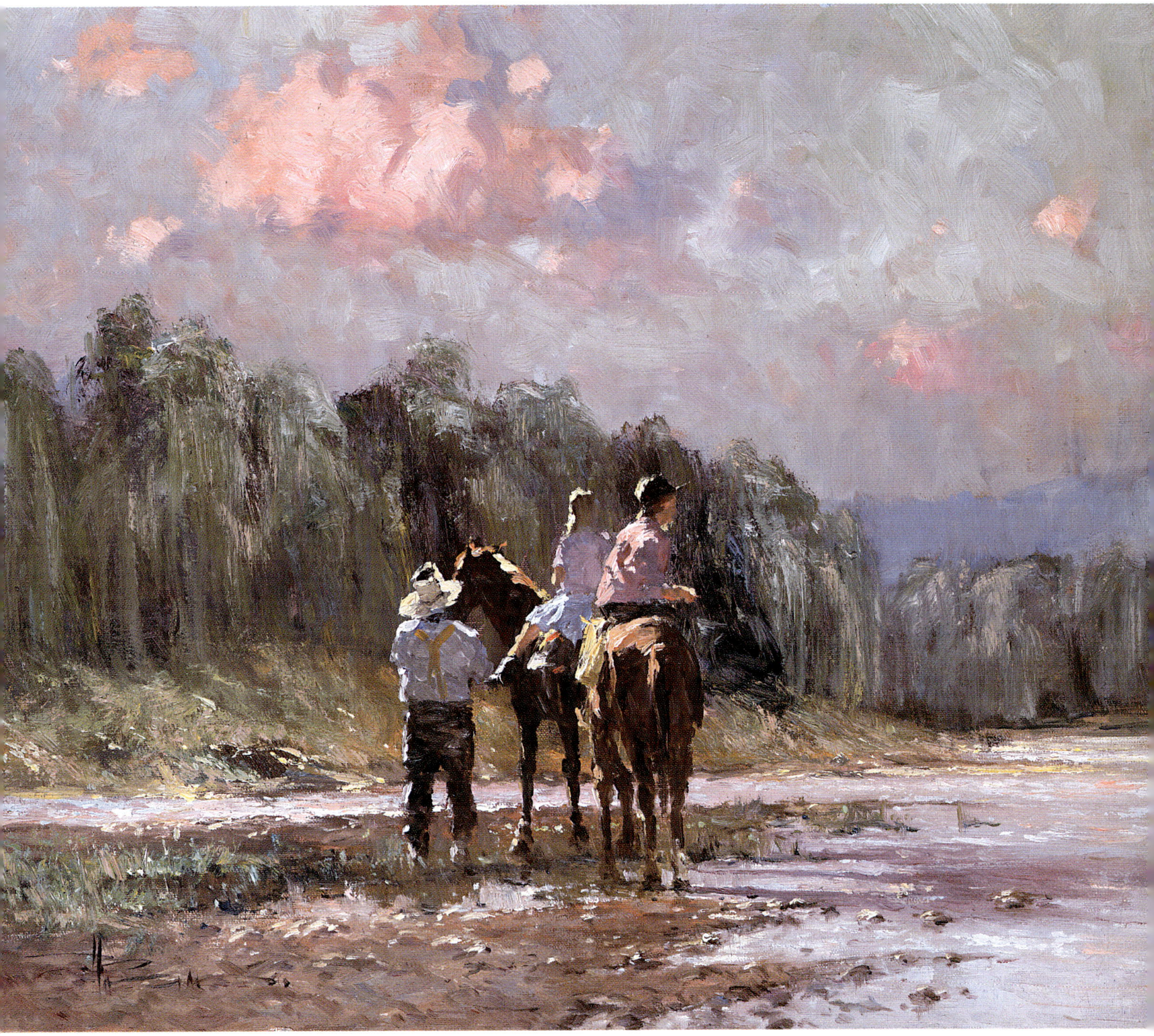

STOCKMEN'S TEA-BREAK

(Nappa Merrie, south-western Qld)

I found these two stockmen having their morning tea-break near a place called Nappa Merrie in the far south-west of Queensland. You'll almost need a magnifying glass to find Nappa Merrie on the map, but it's about 100 kilometres east of Innamincka, which is over the border in South Australia.

Nappa Merrie is on Cooper's Creek, a name tragically associated with the explorers Burke and Wills, and all around here is called the 'Channel Country.' It can be hot, merciless land in the bad, dry years, but in good years, when there's been enough rain on the soil, it can be fine cattle-fattening country.

At any time of the year, even under the best conditions, this is no place for the unprepared and unwary traveller. It's the kind of country that killed Burke and Wills 130 years ago and it probably hasn't changed much since then. Getting lost here is not highly recommended.

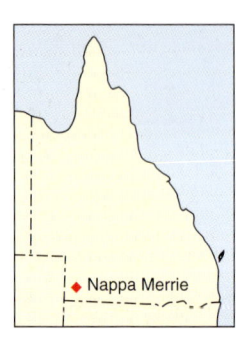

59

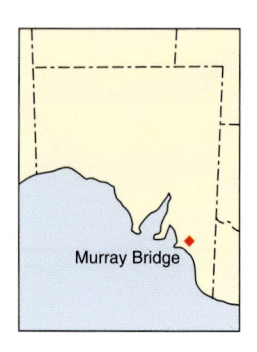

MURRAY BRIDGE ANGLING CLUB
(Murray Bridge, SA)

Murray Bridge is a very pretty town on the lower Murray River about 80 kilometres south-east of Adelaide. It was quite a famous river port until road and rail transport took over from the river trade. Originally called Mobilong, it became popularly known as Murray Bridge when a mighty bridge was built across the Murray in the 1870s. Officially, though, it was Mobilong until 1924. The creeks running off the lower Murray in the town are popular fishing spots for the local children.

61

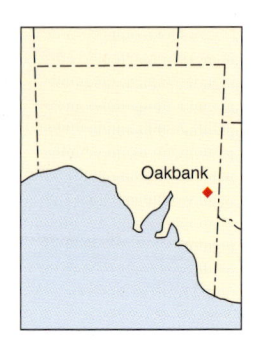

PICNIC AT OAKBANK

(Oakbank, north-east of Adelaide, SA)

Every Easter Monday at Oakbank in South Australia they run the famous Great Easter Steeplechase, one of the most gruelling horse races in Australia. The Easter racing carnival at Oakbank attracts huge crowds and the meetings on the Saturday and Monday are conducted in a picnic atmosphere with families selecting spots among the gum trees that surround the racing arena. But even without a racing carnival going on, Oakbank is always a popular picnic spot, especially for Adelaide families seeking a break from the bustle and noise of city life.

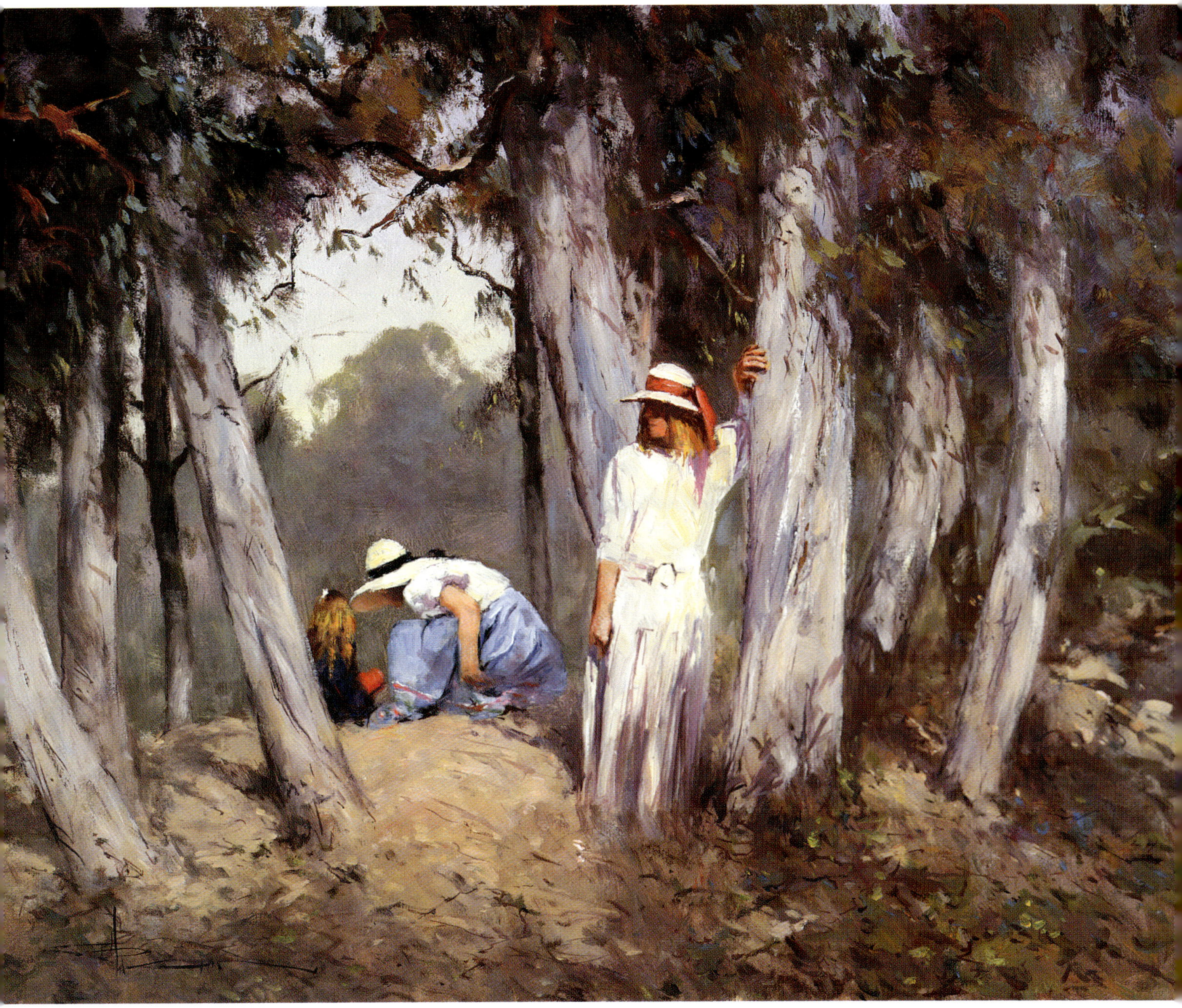

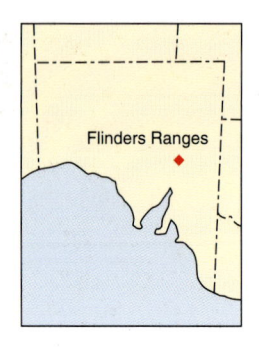

AROONA VALLEY
(Flinders Ranges, SA)

This is one of the most remarkably scenic valleys to be found anywhere in Australia. To get to it you have to travel north of Wilpena Pound in South Australia's Flinders Ranges. The valley was made famous in the late 1920s by the wonderful paintings of Sir Hans Heysen and, in fact, the west border of this valley is called Heysen Range in his honour.

The concept for this painting occurred to me when I was trekking through Aroona Valley and contemplating Heysen's obsession with painting the gum trees of the Flinders Ranges. My reverie was suddenly disturbed by an invasion of colourful galahs and I was struck by the vivid contrast of the explosion of colour, set against the timeless solemnity of the grey gum-tree trunks.

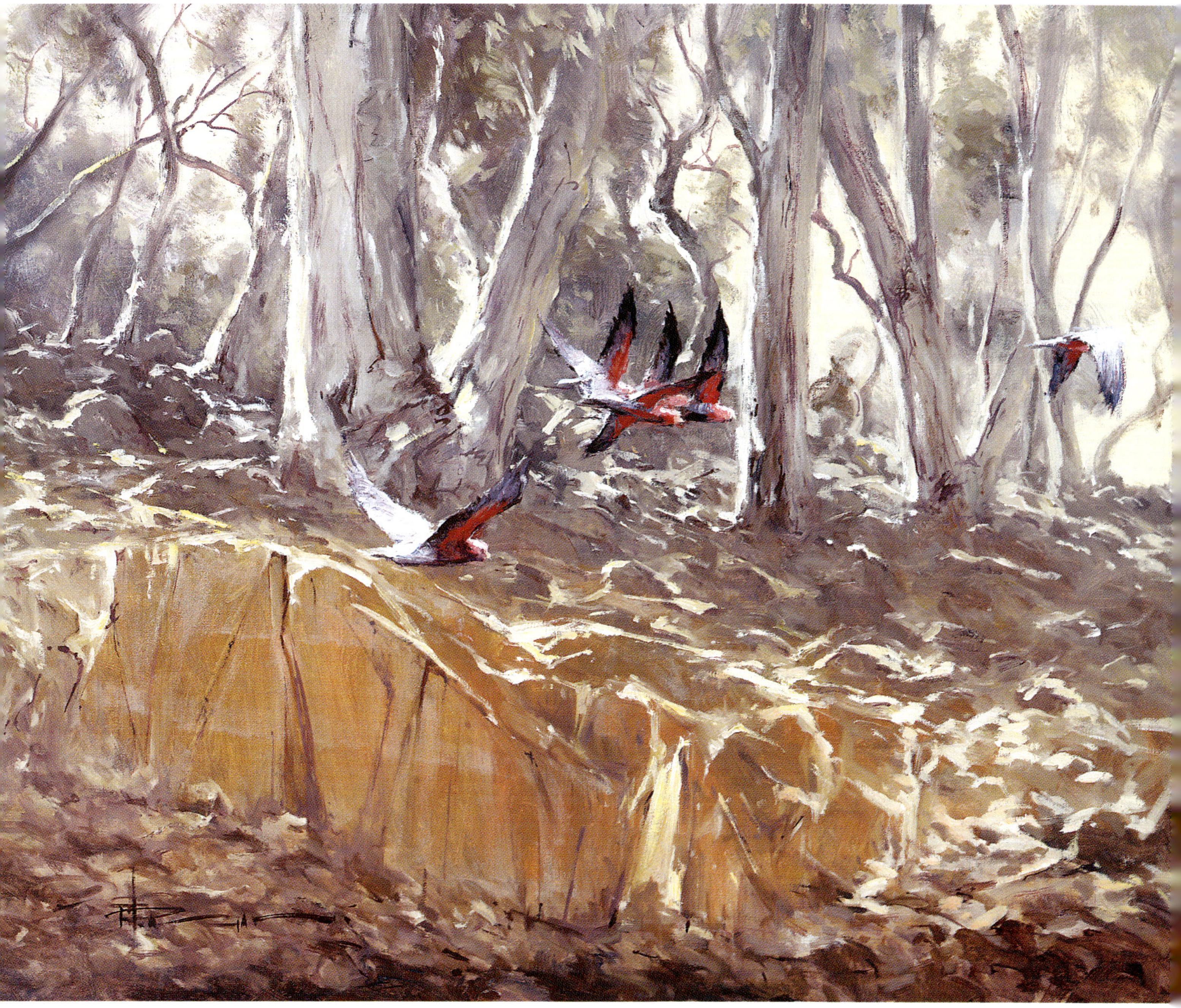

SOFALA
(Central NSW)

If you've ever been interested in gold prospecting as a hobby the name Sofala should ring a bell. It's the name of a famous town in South Africa where it's known as "The Gateway to the Goldfields."

That's how come the Sofala in central NSW, next door to the historic goldfield town of Hill End, got its musically sounding handle way back in the early 1850s when there was one heck of a gold rush in these parts. A bit later on in 1872 the incredible Holtermann Nugget was found at Hill End. It was one of the biggest nuggets ever unearthed and it contained a massive 93 kilograms of gold so, not surprisingly, almost overnight some 40 hotels sprung up in nearby Sofala.

Today, the hordes of gold prospectors have long since departed and now there's just the one pub left, the Royal run by dear old Eileen Farrell who's in her late 70s at time of writing. Eileen took over the Royal in 1955 and she's been running it all on her own since her husband died a few years ago. The Royal and a few other buildings remain, most of them faded and empty and merely mute reminders of a time when the town was once noisily and exuberantly gripped by gold fever.

"There's still plenty of gold out there in the creeks running off the Turon River," says Eileen. "Some of the locals are always hanging around the creek banks with their pans and we get lots of tourists and lots of hobby prospectors turning up here at weekends. They've all got that same mad glint in their eyes and they all think they'll find another Holtermann Nugget one day. Once they get the fever they never really get rid of it for the rest of their lives."

But even if you don't find any gold in the creek beds around Sofala on your visit to this quaint old town you'll still strike it rich just by sitting and having a yarn to this wonderful old lady, Eileen Farrell. And make sure to stay for a meal because she serves the biggest, juiciest rump stakes this side of the Darling Downs.

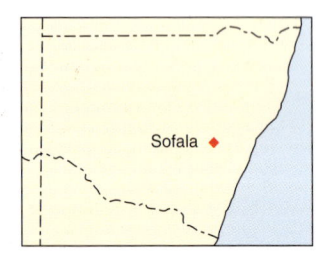

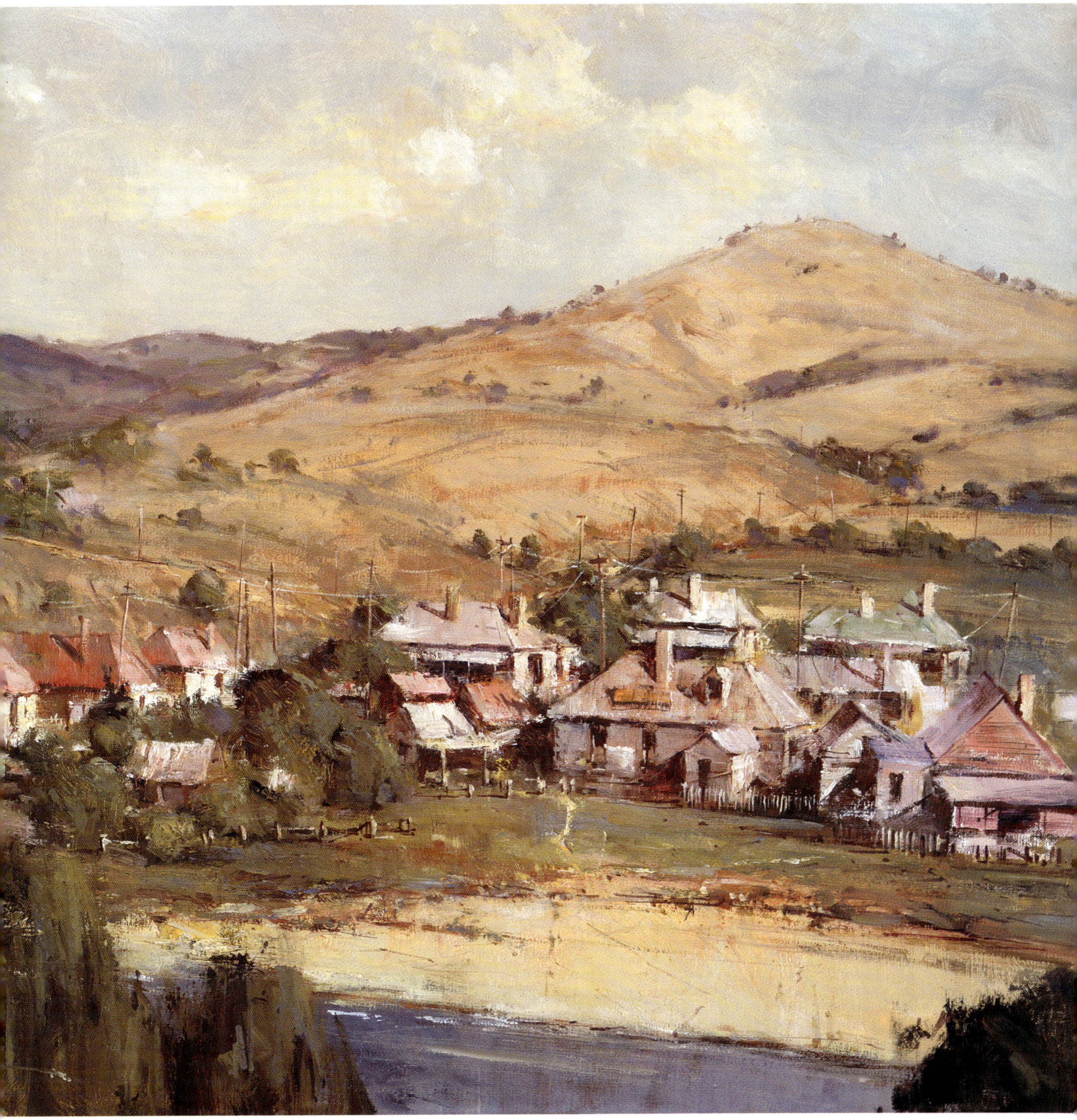

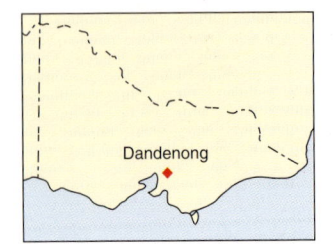

FLASH OF COLOUR

(Dandenong Ranges, Vic.)

During the 1980s I made several painting expeditions to the Dandenong Ranges which are mostly to the south east of Melbourne and every time I've been to the Dandenongs I've nurtured a wild hope of coming across a lyrebird. The Sherbrooke Forest here is said to be one of the more likely areas to find these unique Australian birds, which are world famous for their remarkable mimicking abilities, and countless artists have found them there. But I guess I make such a racket as I'm blundering through the bushes the wily lyrebird can hear me coming from miles away and wisely gives me a wide berth. Still, there's always the opportunity for a beautiful consolation prize whenever I go to the Dandenongs and on this particular excursion I came across one of Australia's most exotically colourful birds, the king parrot. I was lucky even to catch a glimpse of him because, unlike most of the parrot species, the king parrot doesn't seem to be at all relaxed in the presence of the human species. This character took off in startled flight as soon as he spotted me coming into view from behind a clump of gumtrees.

But what a wonderful image he left for me, fleeting though it was. It was a full grown bird and I could tell it was a male because of that distinctive and dazzling flash of almost luminous scarlet on his chest and around the wings. If you look carefully at this painting you'll also discern little splashes of ultramarine on the head and the lower tail. The male king parrot is truly an artist's dream, but not so the female of the species. She's mostly the one colour green all over.

The old Dandenong Ranges still manage to maintain an extraordinary variety of birdlife despite the fact that the outer suburbs of Victoria's capital city have now reached the very foothills of the ranges. And as a direct result of the increased human population so close to the ranges the problem of feral cats has dramatically increased. I read recently that a feral cat is capable of killing up to 100 wild birds a week, so I certainly hope the schemes for de-sexing cats and getting bells attached to cat collars is introduced as fast as possible.

Just the tinkle of a tiny bell would be enough to give beautiful creatures like this king parrot that split second warning he needs to fly off.

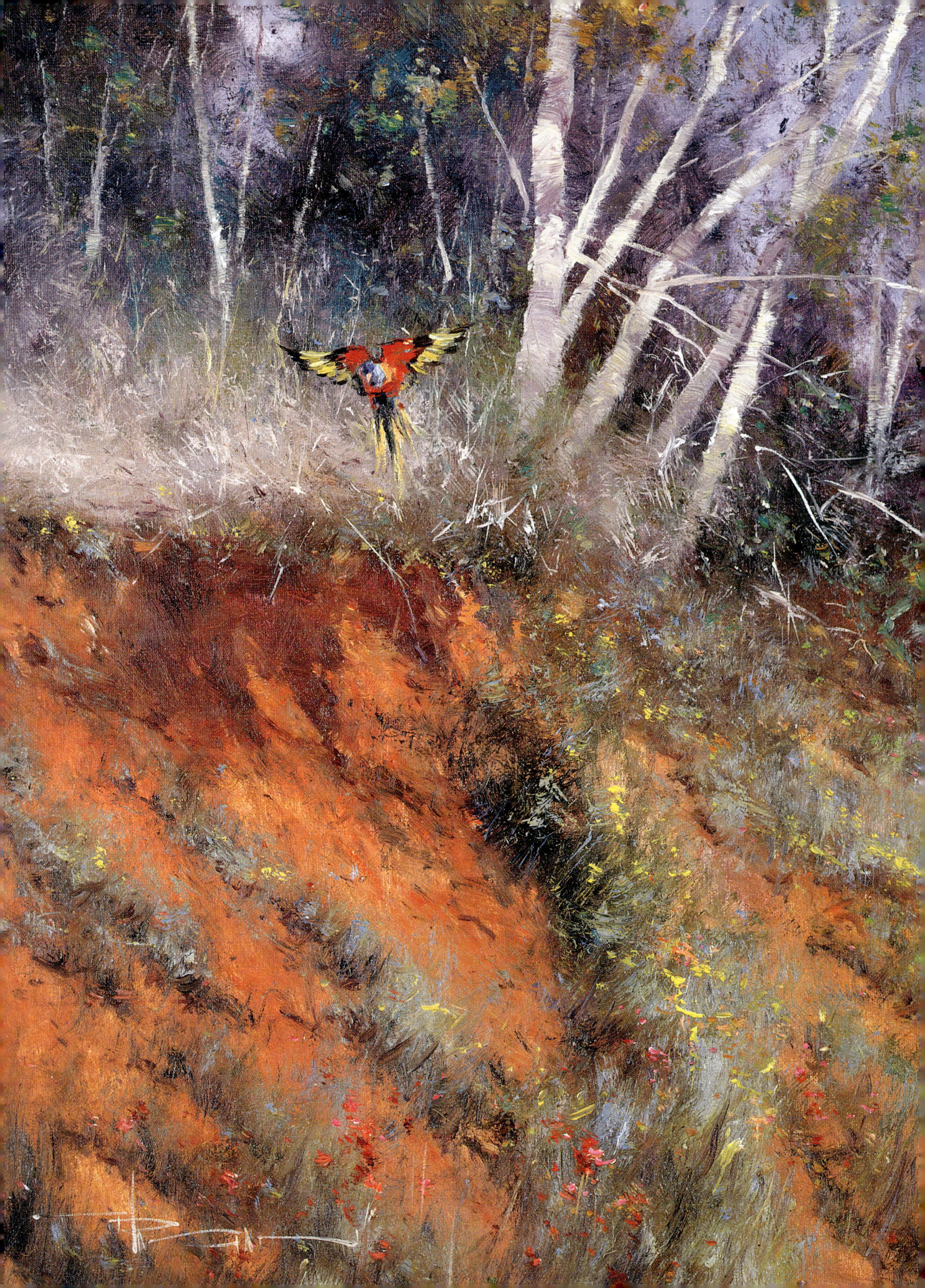

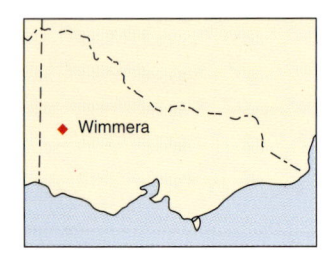

THE CLYDES

(Wimmera District, Vic.)

In Australia today there are around 400,00 horses. This may seem like a lot of horses, but sixty years ago the horse population in the country was more than two-and-a-half million. over the last six decades the working horse has gradually been replaced by mechanical power—the distinctive smell of a horse being replaced by petrol and diesel fumes and carbon monoxide. Working horses, such as therse magnificent Clydesdale giants hauling a load of hay in the Wimmera area of north-western Victoria, are a rare spectacle today. Happily, a few big business houses around Australia have begun using draught horses again, if only for advertising promotions.

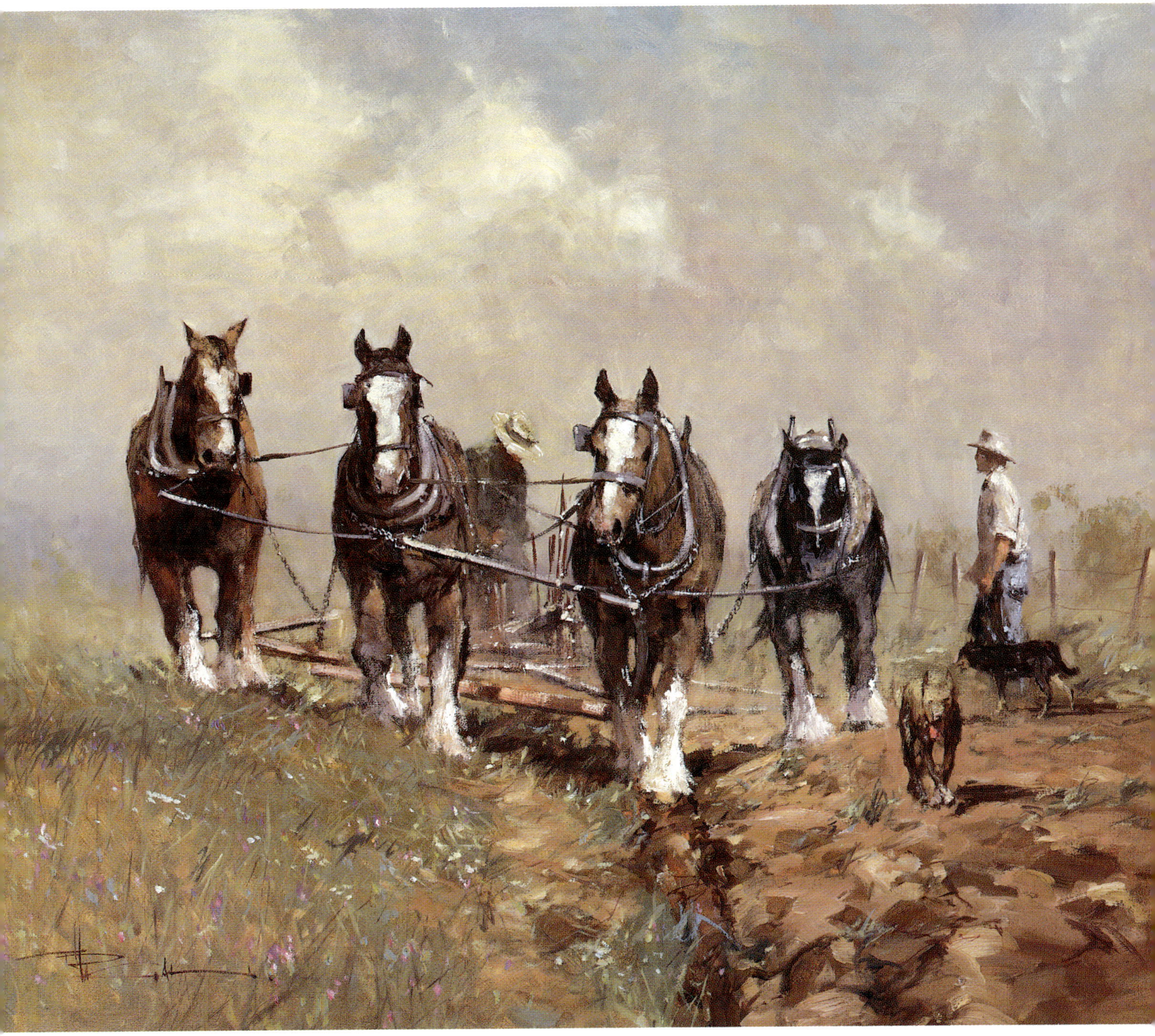

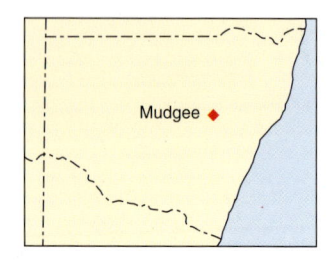

SKEWBALD'S TIME OUT

(Near Mudgee, NSW)

"Old Skewbald was a racehorse
And I wish he was mine
He never drank water
He only drank wine"

I'm always reminded of those funny words from that old country song whenever I come across a skewbald in the bush, although I strongly doubt, from the rotund looks of this particular skewbald that he ever got anywhere near a racetrack in his life.

I found this one on a large property near Mudgee in the central south-east part of New South Wales and to my surprise it was owned and ridden by the property manager and not his son - the boy in the background in this painting sitting on top of a nuggety little bay pony. Normally when skewbalds or piebalds are born the kids on the farm fight over which one is going to keep it as a pet, so consequently it's a little unusual to see a multi-coloured horse being ridden around by an adult.

Incidentally, as I've always understood it, a skewbald is defined as a horse with a combination of white and any other colour except black, and is not to be confused with a piebald, which is specifically a black and white horse. In any case, the skewbald in this painting is having a well-earned rest and cooling his heels in a stream running off the Cudgegong River. This spot is a very tranquil setting today, but it was certainly a scene of much bustling activity back in the 1860s. In those exciting far off days thousands of miners positioned themselves all along the banks of this stream and other nearby rivulets, all intensely busy with their pans sifting anxiously through the silt for glittering signs of gold dust or little nuggets.

Some nuggets found in the hills around here weren't so little. In fact, the Holtermann Nugget, the biggest reef nugget of them all, was gouged from the ground at Hill End which is just on the other side of "them thar hills" in this painting.

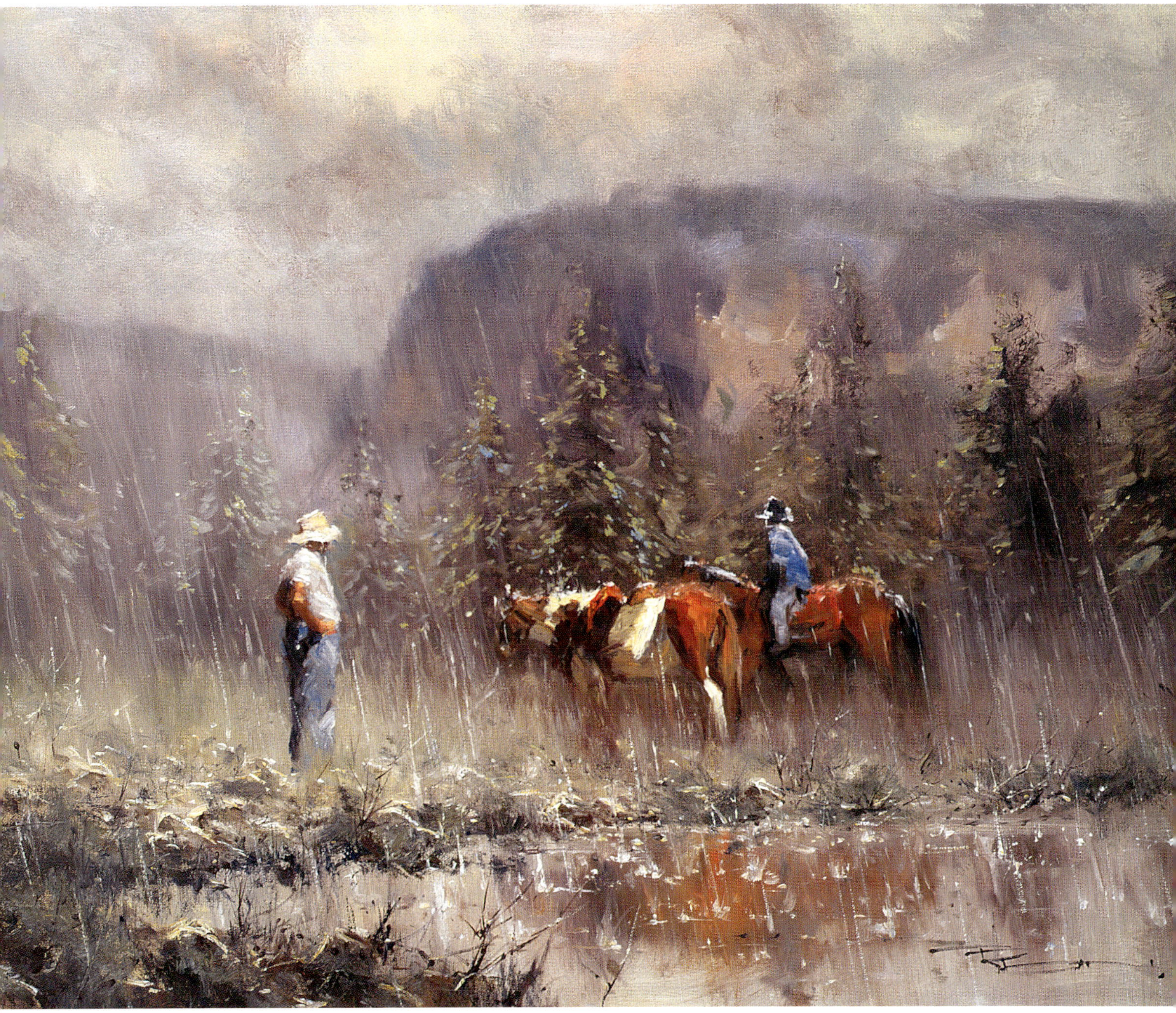

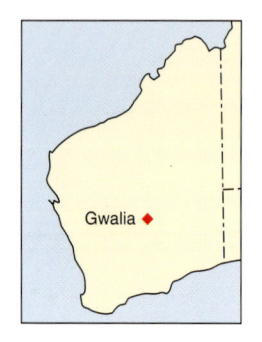

THE TOWN GOES WILD

(Gwalia, WA)

Gwalia, a gold-mining town in the south-east of Western Australia, has only one serious claim to fame — a future American President, Herbert Hoover, actually worked here in 1897 as a mining engineer. Hoover became President much later in 1929 and, apparently, there was quite a celebration in Gwalia on the day of his inauguration.

All the gold mines eventually closed down at Gwalia, but many of the old buildings remain. In this painting, I've turned the clock back to try and recapture the exuberance and roistering that must have occurred outside this old hotel back in 1929 on the day the news came through via the telegraph wires that a former mining engineer, who once worked in one of the remotest towns in the world, had become President of the United States of America.

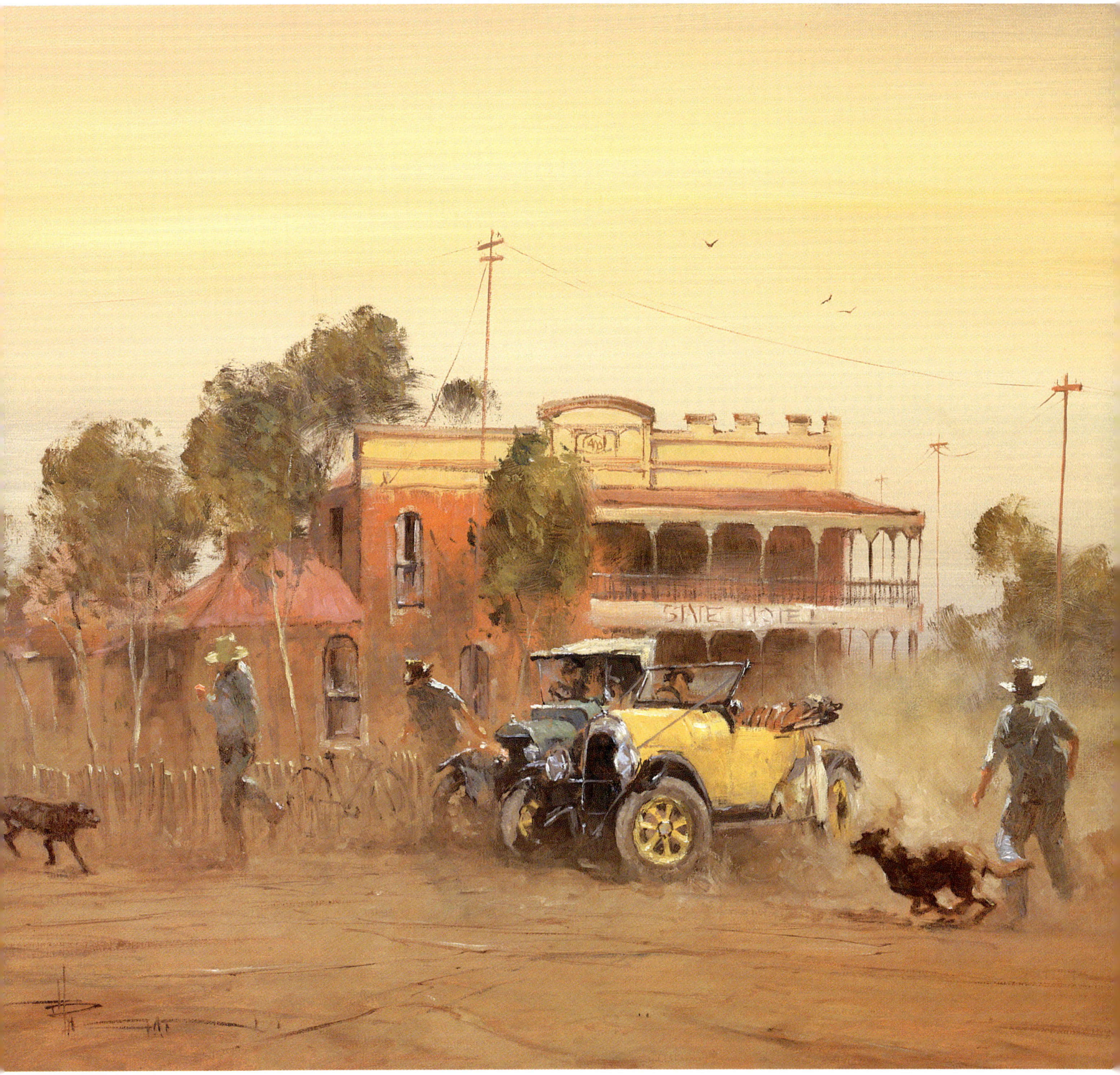

THE OPENING BATSMAN
(Cue, WA)

Some of Australia's greatest Test cricketers first wielded a bat in the back streets of some of the smallest towns in this country. Perhaps the stylish young batsman here at Cue in Western Australia is going to become another Allan Border.

Cue is an old gold-mining town, about 650 kilometres by road north-east of Perth, and today it's not much more than a dot on the map. The gold ran out during the 1930s and when the gold started to disappear so did most of the population. Now only a few hundred people are left in Cue, but it's not in danger of becoming a ghost town, because it's on the Northern Highway and tourists like to stop there to inspect the wonderful old buildings still standing. Some of them, especially the government buildings, are still in use.

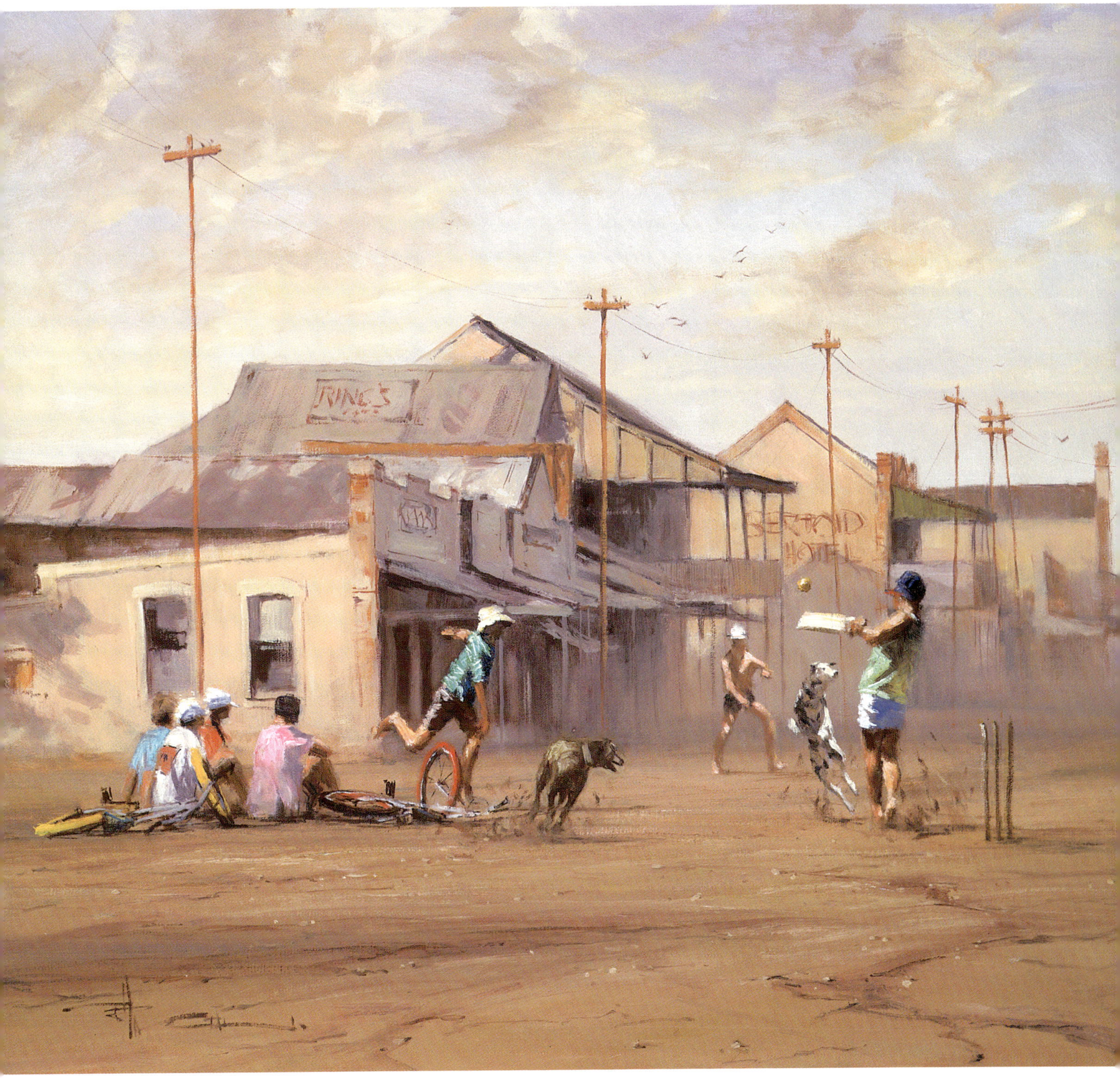

REFLECTIONS ON THE SWAN

(Close to Perth, WA)

The Swan is one of the few major rivers in Australia that is not named after some early colonial political figure and the simple reason for this is because it was given its name long, long before Australia was colonised by the British.

Back in 1697 (would you believe?) the Dutch explorer Willem de Valmingh and some of his crew rowed about 80 kilometres up the Swan and he was the first white man to actually prove the existence of black swans. Up until then Europeans had only heard of them in mythological terms, such as pink elephants, perhaps.

Anyway, old Willem de Valmingh was quite sure no-one would believe his story about black swans, so he sent some of his crewmen out to rugby-tackle a few of them and the captured swans were duly transported all the way back to Holland. Frankly, I was almost beginning to doubt the existence of black swans myself when I set up my easel on the banks of the river, about 40 kilometres out of Perth, to start this painting because not one single, solitary swan — black, white or brindle — put in an appearance in the four or five hours I sat there.

Happily, a stray horse came along and contendedly contributed its reflection onto the Swan's receptive surface and that explains why there's a horse but not one swan in this painting of Western Australia's most famous river.

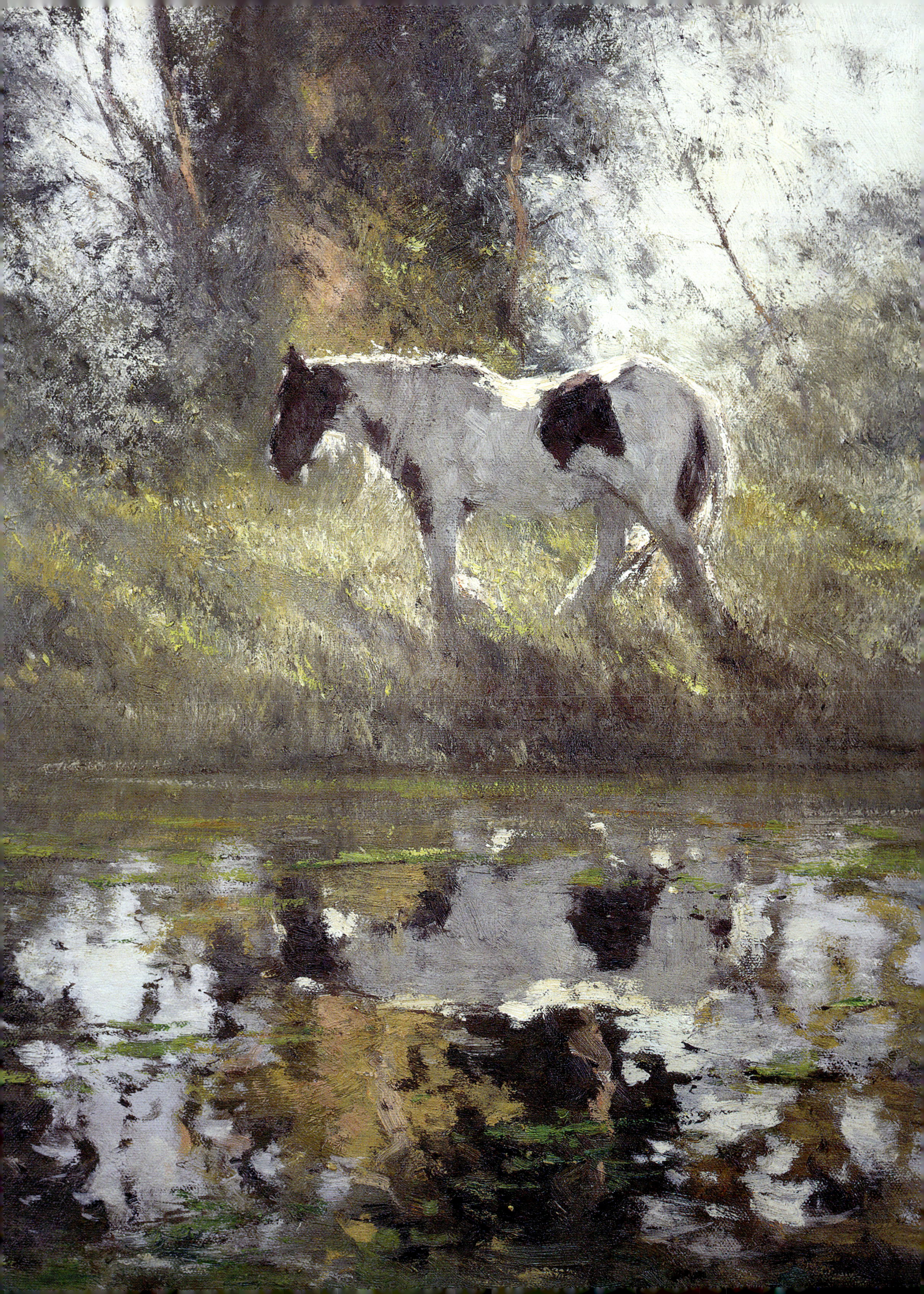

THE EXPLORERS

(Byron Bay, NSW)

There's a pretty little beach about halfway between Brunswick Heads and Byron Bay on the far north coast of New South Wales and it's probably got a name recorded somewhere on the local council charts, but I couldn't find a handle for it anywhere on my roadmaps, so I've just called it No-name Beach. Not exactly poetic, but I'm a painter not a poet. The little boy and the little girl haven't been here before and they're doing a spot of exploring the way kids always do as soon as their little feet hit the sand on our coastal beaches.

They're too young to know it, but this beach, being so close to Byron Bay, is just about the most easterly point of Australia and that means that people living around here see the sun come up before anyone else on the entire continent — Byron Bay locals are quite proud of this indisputable fact and very quickly let visitors know all about it. By way of a happy accident, Byron Bay is very aptly named because it takes a poet of Byron's stature to describe the scenic wonders of this glorious subtropical area of Australia with its lush forests, rolling mountains and secluded little beaches such as the subject of this painting.

But, unfortunately, Byron Bay was actually named by Captain Cook in honour of Commander Byron, a famous English seaman of the late 18th century. Pity about that, because this beautiful section of Australia truly deserved to be named after one of the world's most admired poets. And if that had been the case then he would certainly have had Byron Bay in mind when he wrote:

"There is a pleasure in the pathless woods
There is a rapture on the lonely shore
There is society where none intrudes
By the deep sea, and music in its roar
I love not Man the less, but Nature more."

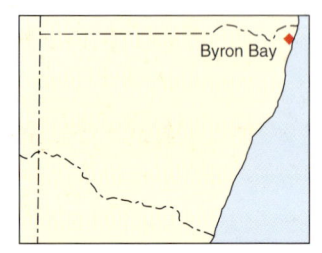

81

SPIRIT OF AUSTRALIA

(Off Point Loma, San Diego, USA)

In the 1980s Australia won and then lost the America's Cup, the Holy Grail of yachting, but there was never any doubt that we would keep trying until one glorious day that famous Auld Mug would be brought back to us.

Iain Murray, the amiable Aussie yachtsman who sailed Kookabura II in our unsuccessful defenseof the Cup off Fremantle in 1986, performed a financial miracle in raising $25 million, mostly from ordinary well-wishing Australians, in his gallant quest to win back the cup with his magnificent racing yacht, Sprit of Australia.

That sum $25 million is certainly a lot of money, but it was chickenfeed compared to the tens of millions poured into the syndicated backing most of the other yachts competing in the 1992 America's Cup series. Iain Murray had a team of just 31 crew and technicans working on Spirit of Australia, whereas the American defender's crew and technical team totalled just over 200.

In terms of money and manpower the odds were hopelessly stacked against them, but the boys on board the two Australian yachts at the 1992 Cup Defence never ever stopped trying. They gave it everything they had, and more.

I went to San Diego on a special assignment to paint all the competing yachts from several nations in the 1992 America's Cup series and even though I intended to be completely unbiased, it was really quite impossible. I just couldn't help myself putting a touch of undisguised patriotic feeling into my work on the two Australian yachts, and I think that's fairly evident in this painting of Spirit of Australia — the people's challenger.

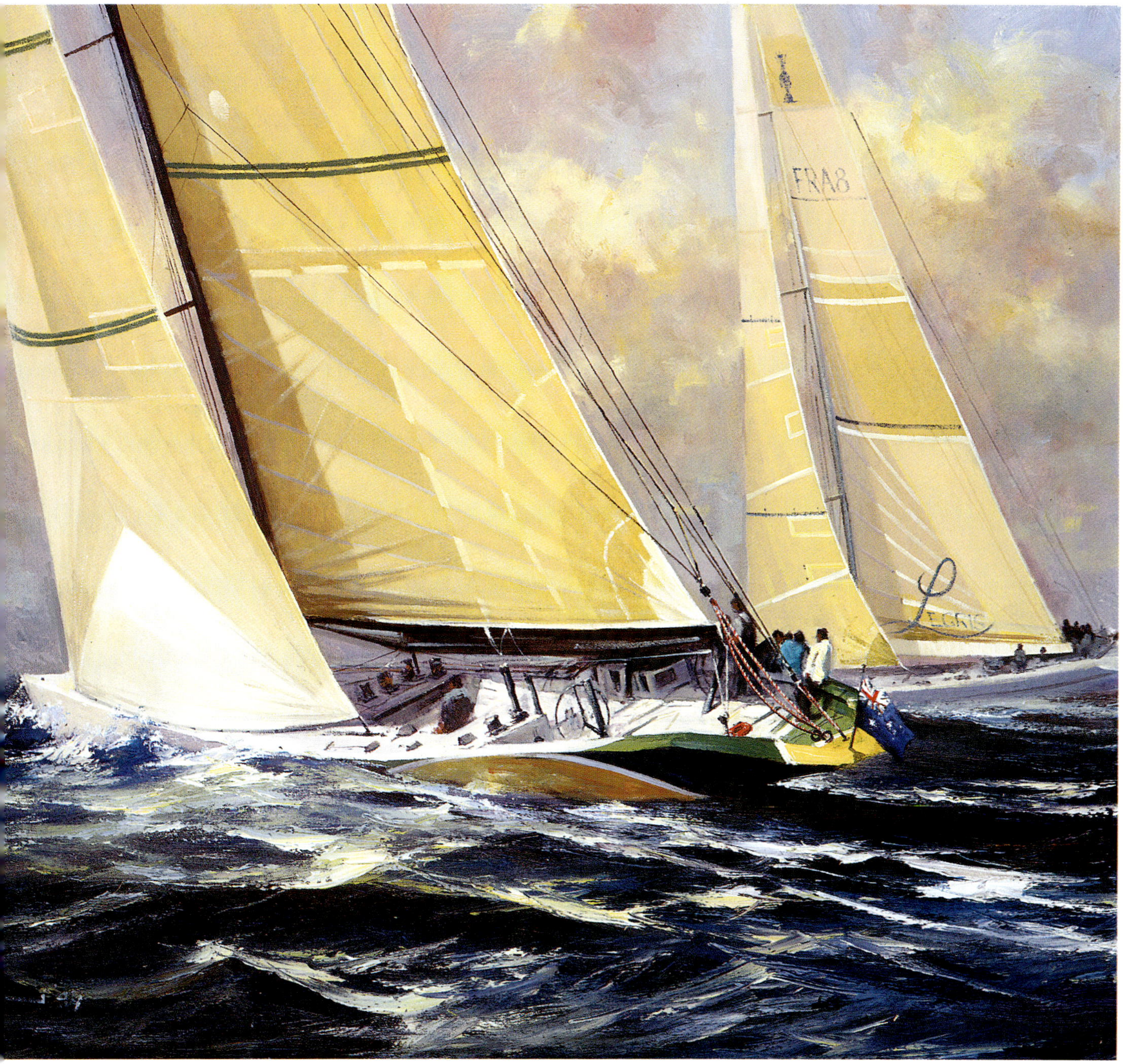
FRA8
LEGRIS

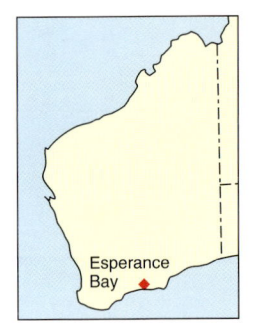

THE YOUNG EXPLORER

(Esperance Bay, Western Australia)

When I happened to spot this little fishing dinghy on the banks of Esperance Bay in Western Australia I couldn't help but be reminded of the very strong French naval connection to Australia's early exploration. The bay was given its name by French explorer Admiral Bruni d'Entrecasteaux after one of his ships L'Esperance when he took shelter here from the mountainous waves of the nearby Great Australian Bight as far back as 1792. There's also a township in the bay called Esperance and more than 2,000 km from here in Tasmania, would you believe, there's another town called Esperance and also a Port Esperance — all of them named after his one ship.

Esperance, in French, I discovered on my visit there, means 'hope,' not 'experience,' as I'd mistakenly believed, so it was at least an educational experience for me to call in on this now little heard of bay and township which, by its name alone, must always remind us of how close we came to being a French instead of English settlement.

Admiral D'Entrecasteaux was exploring the southern coast of Australia in two ships, L'Esperance and Recherche, which means 'research,' in a romantic search of the missing French explorer La Perouse when he decided to duck into the bay for a breather way back in 1792. History records that although the intrepid Admiral had both hope and research going for him he never did find any trace of his fellow explorer Jean La Perouse who had perished when his ship was wrecked in the New Hebrides in 1788.

I just hope the little boy intently exploring the sandy banks of Esperance Bay in this painting is aware of the very interesting history of this tranquil haven on the edge of arguably the most dangerous sealane on the entire Australian coastline.

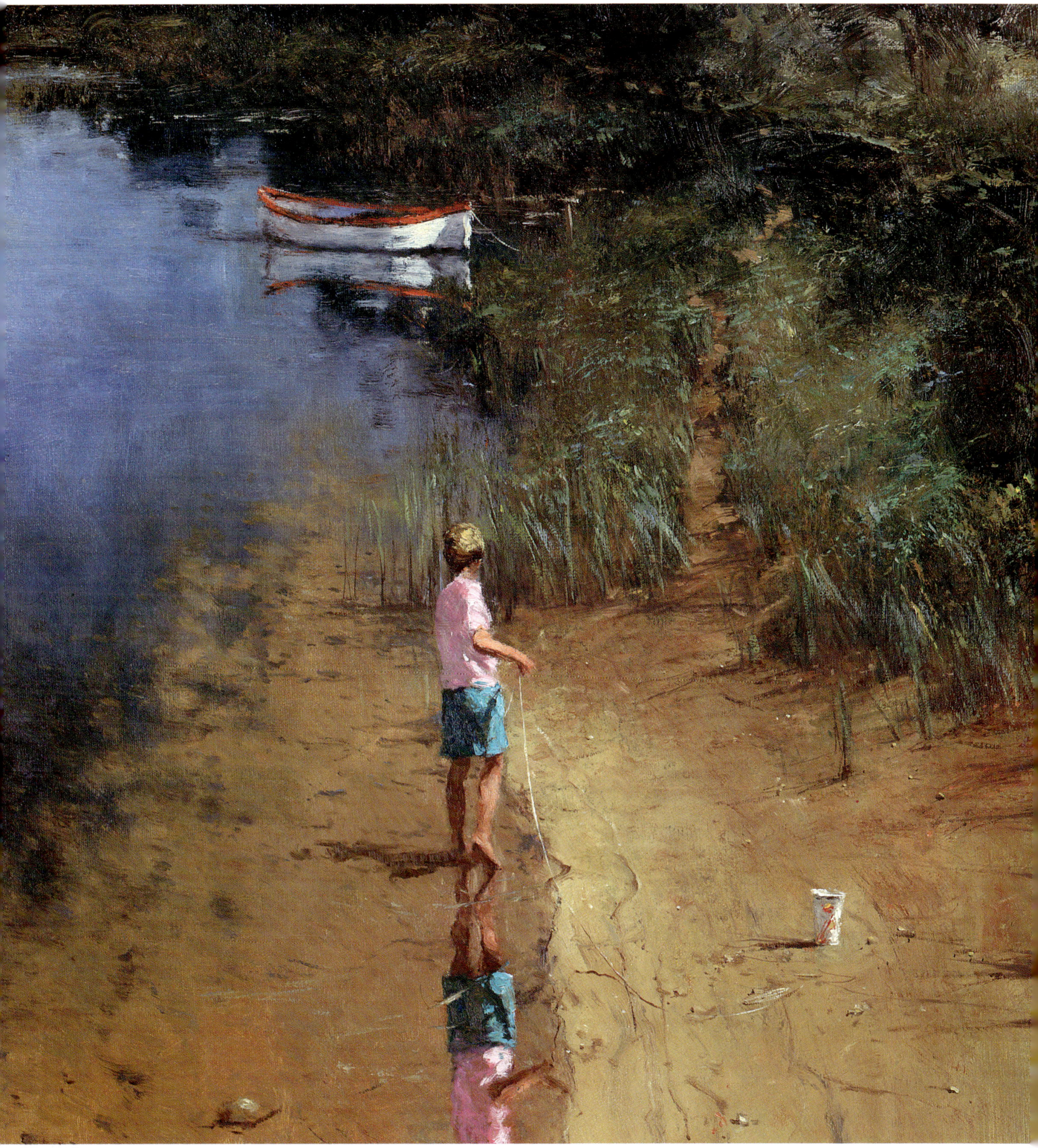

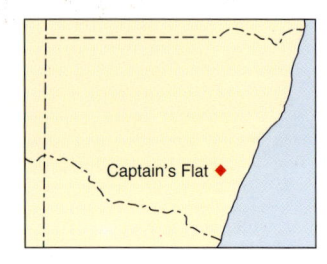

GRASSHOPPER JOE

(Near Captain's Flat, NSW)

Grasshopper plagues are a big worry for Australian farmers every summer when these voracious little insects join up in swarms so vast they almost blacken the sky. But when there's just a few of them about they don't do much damage and country kids like this carefree trio have fun going after them just to see how many they can catch in an hour or so.

This is a scene just outside the small town of Captain's Flat, on the southern tablelands of New South Wales, about 60 km east of Canberra, and the kids here are hunting Gumtree grasshoppers, which as the name suggests are a species that flourish around eucalypt trees. The unusual name, Captain's Flat, intrigued me and after making local enquiries I was informed the town was named after quite an extraordinary character in Australia's early colonial history.

The gentleman concerned was one Francis Rossi and he was a Corsican who somehow held the rank of captain in the British Army before he came out to New South Wales under very mysterious circumstances in the early 1920s.

When Captain Rossi suddenly turned up in Sydney town it was widely rumoured that he'd only come out here to get away from several scandals back in London including an accusation that he'd been involved in the slave trade at Mauritius. Another rumour had him as a discredited witness at the famous trial of Queen Caroline, so with a shady past like that it must have come as quite a shock to Sydneysiders that soon after his arrival he was appointed the colony's first Police Chief.

In spite of his dubious reputation the Captain worked hard establishing the police force and had many innovative ideas, such as the formation of a water police squad on Sydney Harbour and he also recommended higher pay and pensions to attract a better calibre of copper. Eventually, he was awarded large land grants including the flat area where the town of Captain's Flat was built in his honour. But then it was pointed out that not being a British national he wasn't entitled to the land so the old Captain had to give it all back. Pretty tough for him, but at least they didn't change the name of the town.

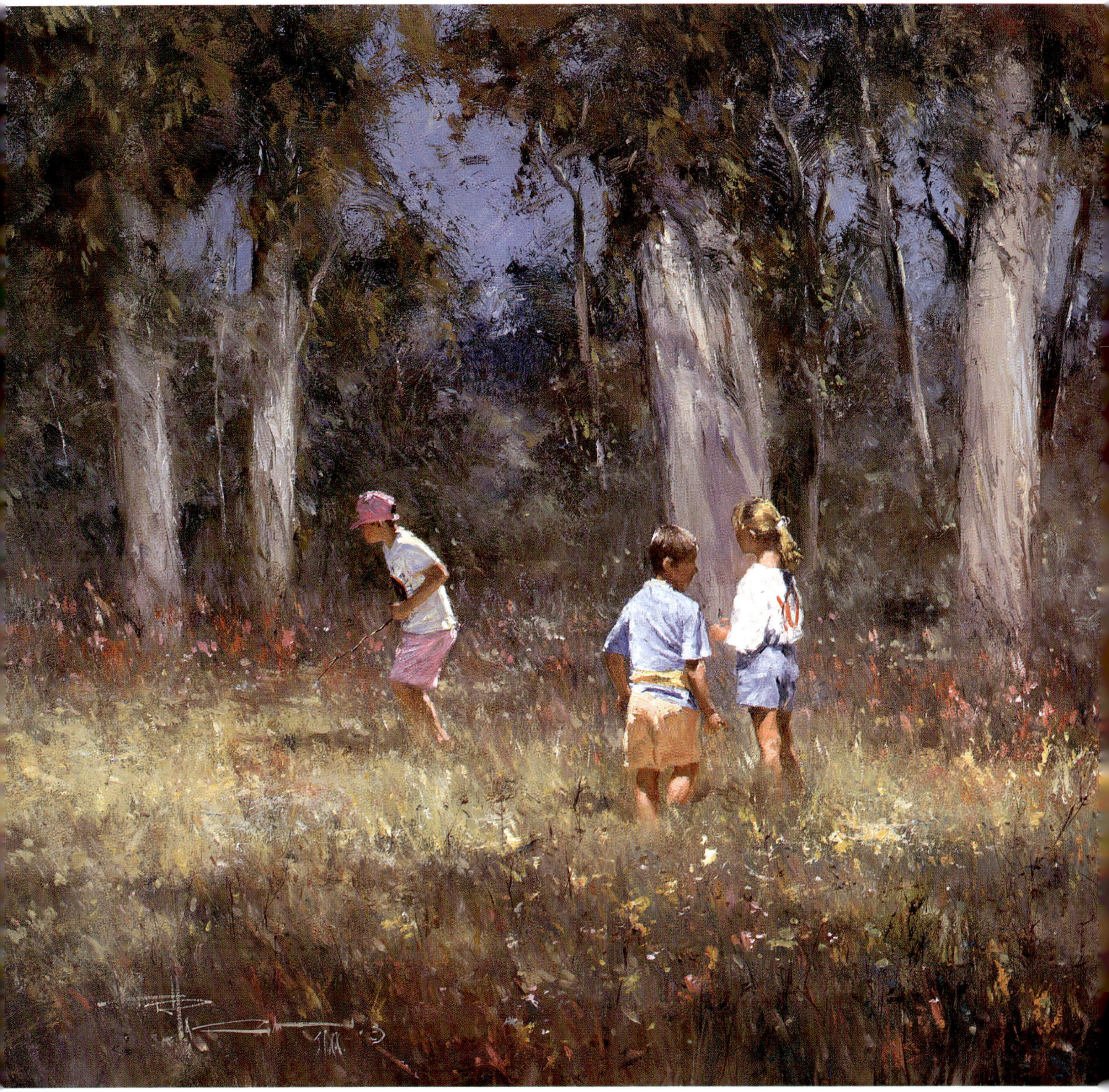

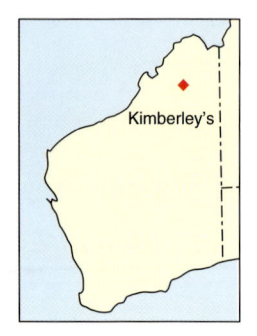

RESTOVER

(Kimberleys, north-eastern WA)

In the United States the vast cattle areas are predominently in the south, way down south in Texas and adjacent States. But in Australia, generally speaking, the opposite geographical situation applies and so Australia's Texas is perhaps the Kimberleys, virtually the roof of the country, in the far north eastern end of Western Australia.

The Kimberleys—what a mellifluous name for cattle country—is an enormous plateau of more than 420,000 square kilometres and in good years it holds around 750,000 head of cattle. Stockmen from the Kimberleys really know their horses and their cattle. They're tough, rugged riders who are often sent out to round up strays in blinding dust storms and fiercely hot temperatures. For a stockman just to announce that he comes from the Kimberleys is all the work-experience credentials he needs.

It was from the Kimberleys in World War Two immediately following the Japanese bombing of Darwin, and with a land invasion a real possibility, that a group of stockmen set off with a huge herd of cattle and then successfully drove them thousands of kilometres to the south. The drive was immortalised in the 1940s motion picture The Overlanders and to this day it is still regarded as one of the great cattle drives in world history.

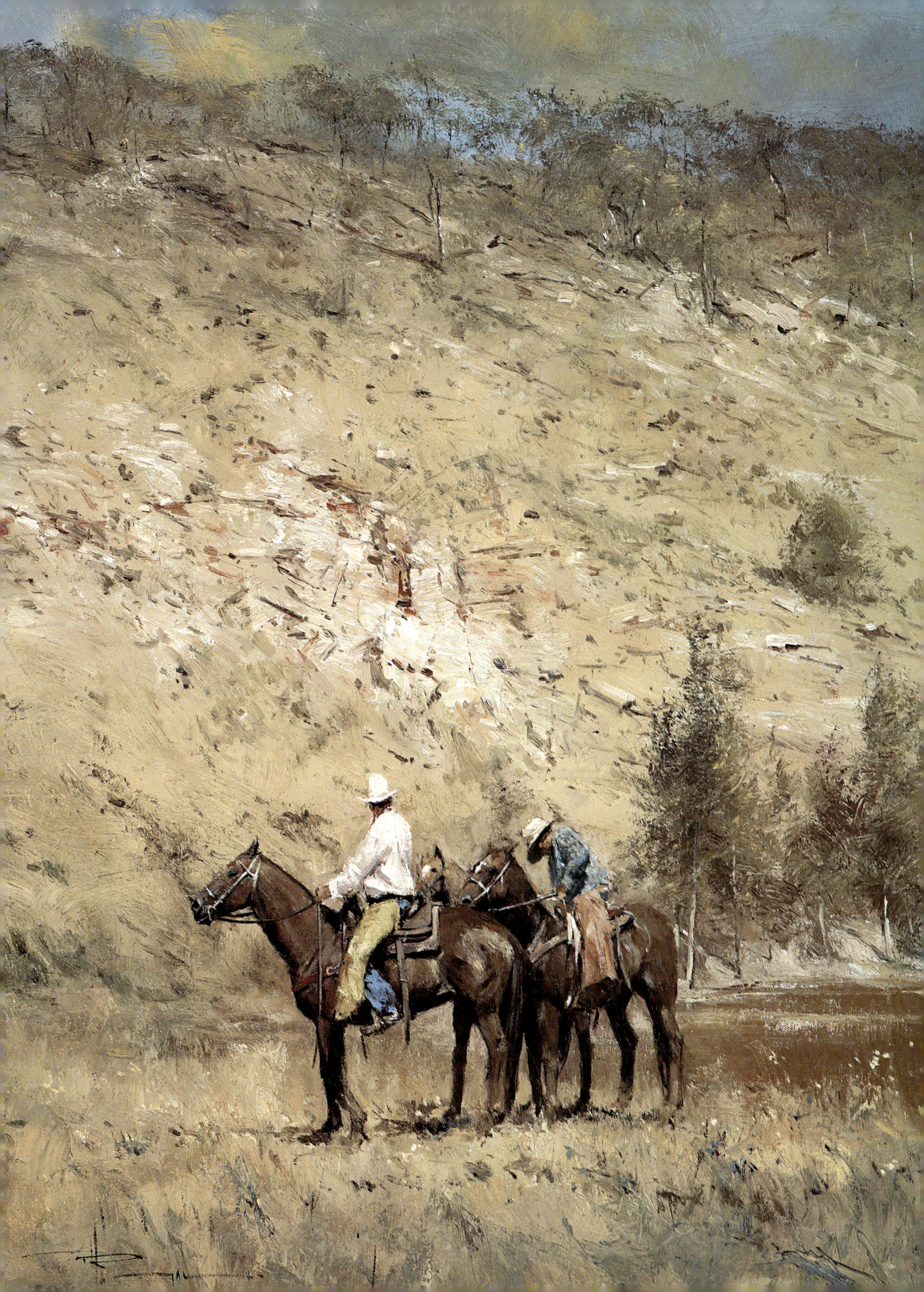

SMALL DISAGREEMENTS
(Yarra River, west of Melbourne, Vic.)

It's fair to say that more disparaging comments have been made about Melbourne's Yarra River than any other watercourse in Australia. "It's the only river in the world that flows upside down," is just a mild example of the many derisive descriptions levelled at the poor old Yarra over the years, invariably by Sydneysiders as part of the traditional Melbourne-Sydney slanging rivalry.

Consequently, the Yarra has gained a reputation for being Australia's muddiest river. And, admittedly, it does look a bit muddy at times, just as all rivers do after there's been some heavy rain about. But its reputation for excessive muddiness is quite undeserved, in my humble opinion. On a good day the Yarra, even as it flows through heavily-populated Melbourne, is quite a beautiful river.

Think of the Yarra and people from other States automatically assume that it starts and ends right there in Melbourne, but, of course the river rises well out of the city in the Great Dividing Range south of Mt. Matlock. It then flows west through delightfully scenic timber and dairying country long before it reaches the city to eventually come out in Port Phillip Bay.

When I came across this section of the Yarra, only about 20 kilometres west of the city centre, it was looking just about as clear as a mountain stream and the grassy banks made an inviting play spot for local children after school. But it seems they must have had a hard time in the classroom on this particular day because they were obviously a bit short-tempered with each other.

A small disagreement was going on over something or other and the little boy has had quite enough. He's stalking away from his sister and she's giving him verbal heaps as he goes off in a huff.

Incidentally, I've checked through the library and discovered that the Yarra gets its name from an Aboriginal word meaning "ever flowing river" and definitely not "river that flows upside down" as Sydneysiders will have you believe.

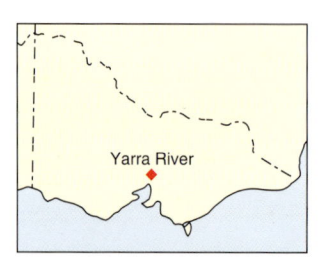

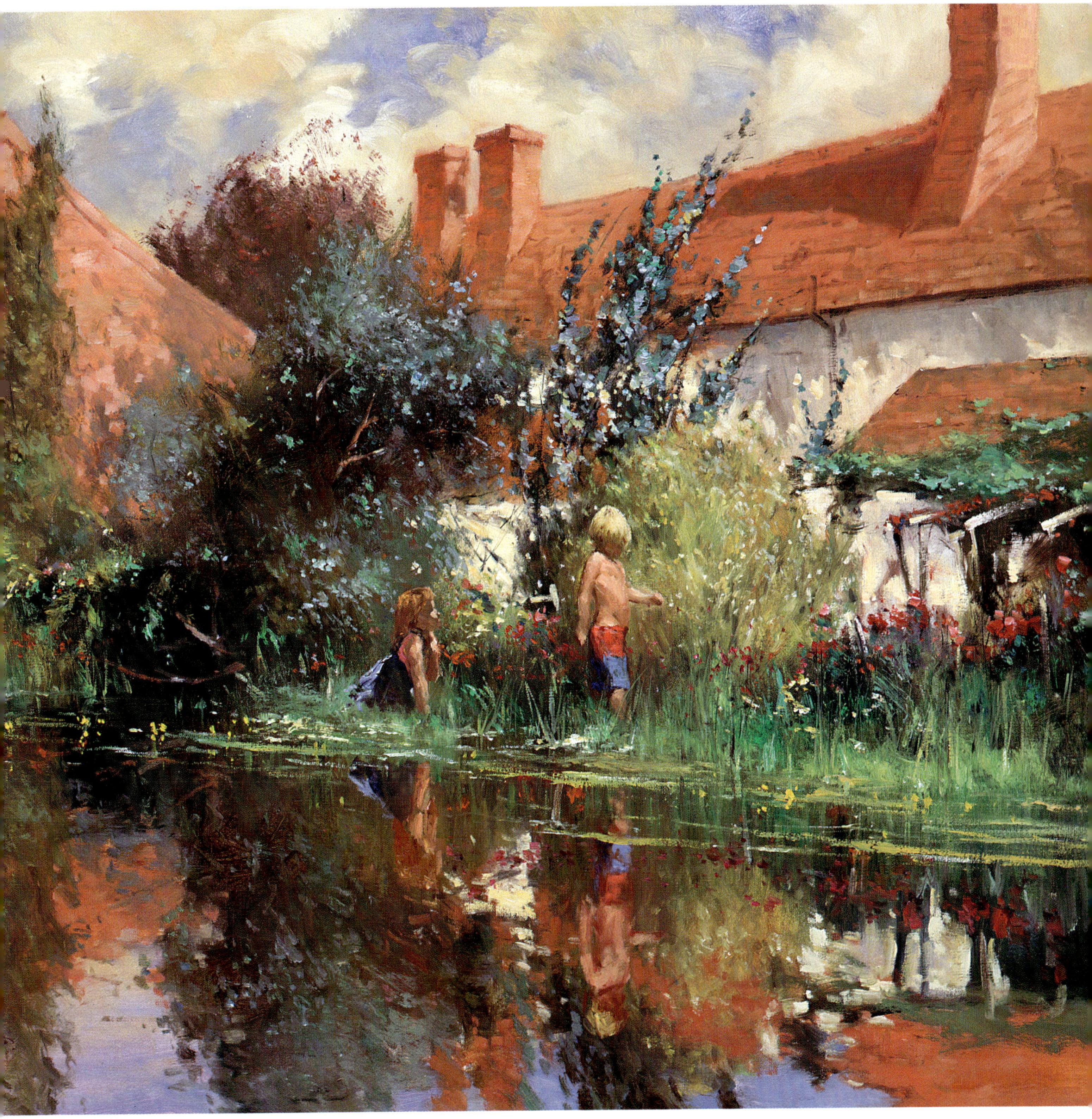

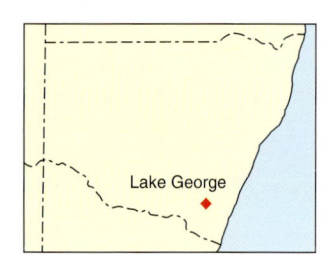

LAKE GEORGE IBISES
(Lake George, ACT)

Marsh birds, such as the graceful ibis, can be found wading in the shallows of lakes, rivers and just about any kind of water catchment area anywhere in Australia. I painted these birds on the edge of the mysterious Lake George in the Australian Capital Territory. The mystery of Lake George, of course, concerns the occasional disappearance of the water, which makes the lake so dry it can be used for grazing sheep. This phenomenon baffled scientists for many years until they decided the water must go into crevasse drains and from there into several subterranean rivers in the area.

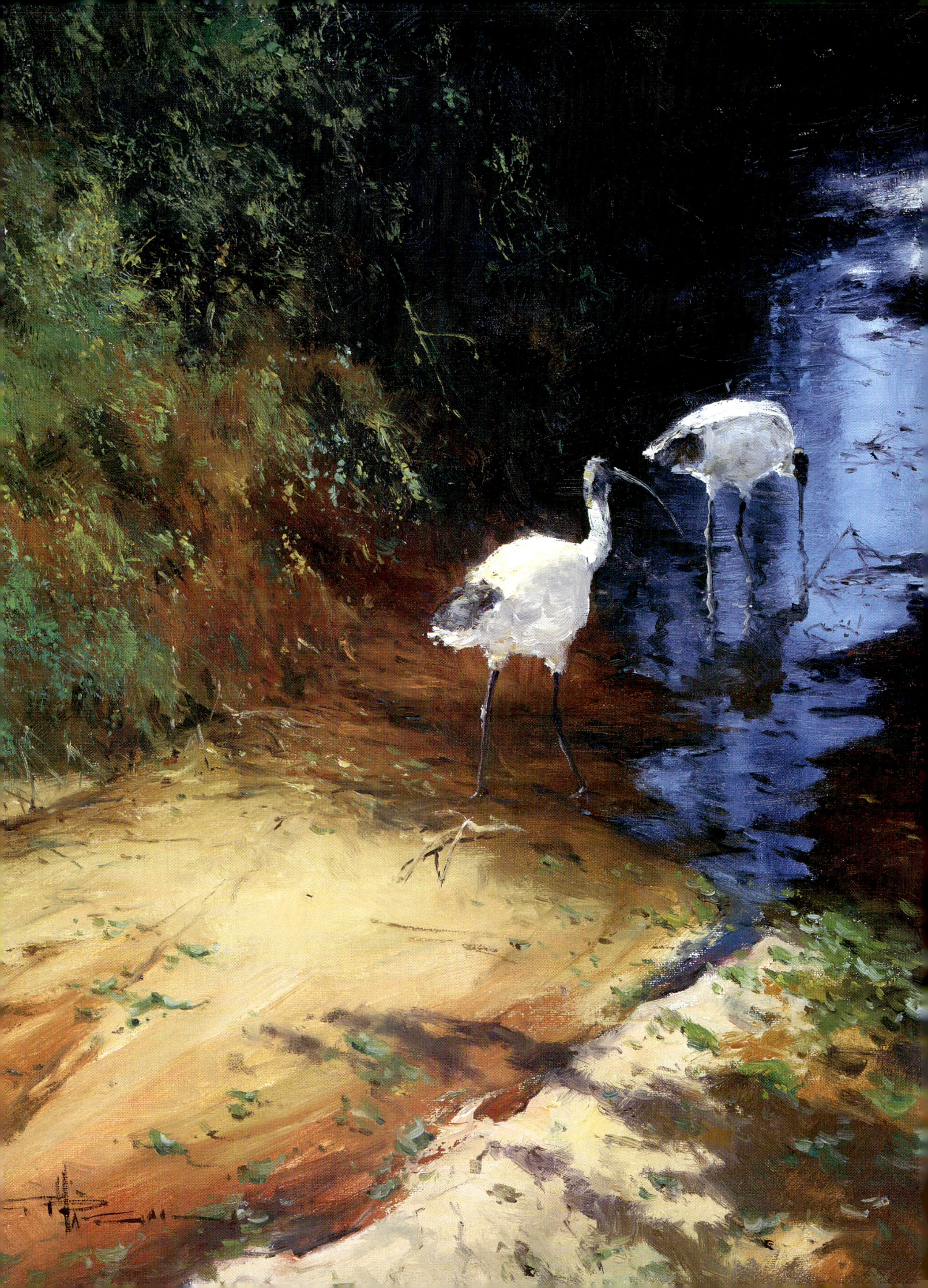

INDEX

(*Italics* indicates a painting.)

Adelaide 60
Aroona Valley 65
Australia II 10

Ballarat Girls 49
Ballarat 48
Billinudgel 15
Billinudgel 14
Black Rock 11
Boonah 16
Boonah Farmhouse 17
The Bridge 23
Brunswick Heads 8, 18
Bulloo Downs 12
Bulloo River 12
Bundaberg 50
Burnie 42
Burnie Boy 43
Byron Bay 11, 80

Cairns 24, 34
Canberra 86
Captains Flat 86
Chillagoe 24
Chillingham 8, 18
Chillingham Adventures 19
The Clydes 71
Coolah 30
Cooper's Creek 58
The Country Meeting 25
Crossing the Bulloo 13
Cue 76
Cunnamulla 52
Cunnamulla Sheep Dogs 52

Dandenong Ranges 68
Darwin 88
Duck Shuffle 51
Dumaresque River 54

Echuca 46
The Enchanting Pond 4–5
Esperance Bay 84
The Explorers 81

Five Day Creek 57
Flash of Colour 69
Flinders Ranges 64

Gone Fishin' with Trigger 11
Gosford 36
Goulbourn River 44
Grasshopper Joe 87
The Gun at Coolah 81
Gwalia 74

Hawkesbury Huckleberries 27
Hawkesbury River 26
Hill End 66, 72
Hobart 42

Kelly Country 39
Kempsey 56
Kimberley's 88
Kookaburra II 3

Lake George 92
Lake George Ibises 93
Lavender Bay 22

Macley River 56
Melbourne 68, 90
Mildura 53
Moment of Authority 55
Mudgee 72
Murray Bridge 60
Murray Bridge Angling Club 61
The Murray Queen 47
Murray River 32, 40, 46
Murwillumbah 8

Nappa Merrie 58
Narrabeen Lakes 20

Oakbank 62
The Old Seedplanter 53
The Openings Batsman 77
Opera House 22

Ovens River 38
Ovens River in Flood 41

Parramatta 20
Perth 78
Picnic at Oakbank 63

Reflections on the Swan 79
Restover 89

Safe Harbour 29
San Diego, U.S.A. 82
Seclusions 35
Seymour 44
Sisters 21
Skewbald's Time Out 73
Small Disagreements 91
Sofala 6, 67
Sofala 66
Spirit of Australia 83
St. Albans 26
Stockmen's Tea Break 59
Swan Hill 32
Sydney Harbour Bridge 22

Tasmania 42
Terrigal 36
Terrigal Pelicans 37
Texas 54
The Town Goes Wild 75
Track Home 33
Turon River 66

Ulladula 28

Wangaratta 40
Wimmera 70

The Yabbie Catcher 45
Yarra River 90
Yarrowee River 48
The Young Explorers 85